Beyond Observations

Beyond Observations

Narratives and Young Children

Susanne Garvis
University of Gothenburg, Sweden

Elin Eriksen Ødegaard
Bergen University College, Norway

and

Narelle Lemon
La Trobe University, Australia

SENSE PUBLISHERS
ROTTERDAM/BOSTON/TAIPEI

A C.I.P. record for this book is available from the Library of Congress.

ISBN: 978-94-6209-966-1 (paperback)
ISBN: 978-94-6209-967-8 (hardback)
ISBN: 978-94-6209-968-5 (e-book)

Published by: Sense Publishers,
P.O. Box 21858,
3001 AW Rotterdam,
The Netherlands
https://www.sensepublishers.com/

Printed on acid-free paper

TABLE OF CONTENTS

LIST OF TABLES AND FIGURES

TABLES

FIGURES

CONTEMPORARY EARLY CHILDHOOD EDUCATION

INTRODUCTION

Over the past few decades, a growing body of literature examining children's perspectives of their own lives has developed, following the emergence of the 'new social studies of childhood' (James et al., 1998) and the children's right discourse (The United Nations Convention on the Rights of the Child, 1989). Children are therefore viewed as social actors who are experts in their own lives and understanding of the world (Kellett and Ding, 2004; Mauthner, 1997). This new approach towards childhood has also meant a methodological shift towards the emergence of 'participatory' research methodologies. Until recently, research was based fundamentally *on* children rather than *for* children and *with* children (Darbyshire et al., 2005; Mayall, 2000; O'Kane, 2000).

This chapter will provide an up-to-date examination of the new directions for contemporary research perspectives, with a specific focus on how the role of children's participation in the research process has evolved. The chapter aims to encourage readers to critically reflect on these new ways of thinking and discuss the future for research with children, with acknowledgement of what narrative research can offer in contemporary times.

CONTEMPORARY THEORIES

There have been many social, economic and technological changes in the late 20th centre and early twenty-first century across the world, resulting in a change of experiences for childhood. For children in developed countries, most children now experience a range of technologies as part of their everyday lives. Books, magazines, television programs, movies, internet sites, food, computer games and collectables are all increasingly connected to children' popular culture (Buckingham, 2000). Popular culture provides many children with a shared frame of reference that is drawn into play with reinvention of characters and plots (Jones Diaz et al., 2007) and contributes to identity construction (Kenway & Bullen, 2001).

These changes have also influenced the way children's learning is viewed. In particular, contemporary perspectives of children's learning are influenced by socio-cultural theory, postmodernism, the sociology of childhood, poststructuralist theory and the reconceptualising early childhood movement. All of these contemporary perspectives recognise the "meaning-making competences of children as a basis for learning" (Malaguzzi, 1998, p. 81). The child is therefore positioned as strong with agency on their own learning within intricate and rapidly changing contexts (Clarke & Moss, 2001; Dahlberg et al., 2007; Gutierrez et al., 2007).

Socio-cultural theory "challenges us to examine our ideas and assumptions about traditional early childhood practices to analyse how relevant and useful these are for children from diverse families and cultures" (Arthur et al., 2012, p. 14). This perspective recognises the family context as the site where children learn 'cultural tools' (Vygotsky, 1978). It is for this reason that the social interactions of family life have become highly significant (Rogoff, 2003). For example, in the family context children will learn about having a meal, interacting with others, shopping and working. Children learn how to look, talk, act and think from participating in the family practices.

Under this perspective, learning differs for each child and needs to be understood within particular cultural and social contexts (Rogoff, 2003). Through engagement with families and communities, children establish their 'funds of knowledge' (Moll et al., 1992), becoming knowledgeable and skilled in ideas that are practised by their family. Social cultural theorists suggest children therefore learn best when the curriculum is connected to their everyday lives.

Postmodernism perspectives identify changes in society while poststructural perspectives recognise transformation for each person (MacNaughton, 2003). Both perspectives explain concepts of 'family' and 'community' as contexts for children's learning. Both focus on social practice through habitus, social capital and social field based on Bourdieu (1993) and/ or 'discourse' based on Foucault (1978).

With a postmodern perspective, there is considered no single pathway of development for every child and that there is no corresponding set of appropriate practices. Some therefore argue that learning should only be understood within local contexts (Grieshaber & Cannella, 2001; MacNaughton, 2003). Postmodern theorists challenge taken for granted assumptions and the privileging of certain domains such as developmental psychology and work to "expand the range of perspectives possible for early childhood education" (Grieshaber & Cannella, 2001, p. 4).

Poststructuralist perspectives "address the complexities of the relationship between the child, the adult and their cultural context...[and] focus attention on the constitutive roles of gender, race, class and disability in children's learning and development" (MacNaughton, 1995, p. 36). Poststructural theorists believe people have agency in their lives, so they are shaped not only by their environment but by their own identities and actions. Both postmodern and poststructural theorists argue that everyone has multiple identities that are socioculturally constructed, shifting and multifaceted (Dahlberg et al., 2007).

The sociology of childhood perspective (James et al., 1998) critiques the term 'development' for its emphasis on the differences between children and adults that result in the views of children as 'needy'. Rather, a sociology of childhood perspective focuses on valuing the child's current experience and understanding. Children are able to take actions and establish their own experiences that will affect their lives (Lehtinen, 2004). Young children are aware of how to understand and make decisions. Learning is therefore focused on competencies, with acknowledgement of the child's strengths, agency and voice. Curtis and Carter (2000, p. xiii) write:

> If we begin to value who children are, not just what we want them to be, a shift happens in the way we think about learning and teaching. Our jobs become more engaging and fulfilling. We also begin to envision a larger purpose for our profession—making children visible and valued for the ways in which it can enrich our humanity and contribute to our collective identity.

This perspective seeks children's perspectives about issues in which they are involved, or issues that impact upon them. The United Nations *Conventions of the Rights of the Child* (United Nations, 1989) and the sociology of childhood offer theoretical support for approaches that regard children are competent commentators on their own experiences where their views are considered valid and reliable and deserve to be taken seriously (Freeman, 1998; Mayall, 2002). From this perspective has grown the importance of researching *with* children and listening to their views (Alanen et al., 2005).

The reconceptualising early childhood movement grew in the 1980s as a critique movement to the dominance of developmentally appropriate practice in the early childhood field. The reconceptualist perspective challenges "dominant knowledges, ideologies and practices" (Jipson, 2001, p. 4). Traditional early childhood understanding such as child development theory and curricula is challenged and critically examined from cultural and historical lens.

One area of reconceptualisation is the image of the child. The concept of a 'universal child' that was constructed through developmental theory has been challenged, critiquing the prevailing view of childhood as a "Golden Age of life" (Dahlberg et al., 2007, p. 49). Cultural artefacts such as books, greeting cards and movies portray children as 'sweet' and 'innocent'. Hilton (1996) suggests this mythological idealised view was laid down at the turn of the 20th century and does not reflect the reality of most children living in a contemporary society.

Children have also been viewed as 'evil' and 'out of control' (Prout, 2003), where the role of the traditional educator is to exercise power and control over children (Woodrow & Brennan, 2001). Another image has been of the child as 'embryo adults'. This image draws on developmental theories and the concept of children becoming an adult. The role of the educator is to facilitate the child's development to becoming an adult. The child is views as a "labour market supply factor" (Dahlberg et al., 2007, p. 49). The three images (innocent, evil and embryo adult) have "shaped dominant discussions, policy and practice" (Dahlberg et al., 2007, p. 43). These views of the child blind us to the lives children lead in a contemporary world and reinforce stereotypes and existing power relations (Woodrow & Brennan, 2001).

Postmodern, poststructuralist, sociology of childhood and the reconceptualist movement challenge the traditional notion of 'childhood' as a universal concept. Rather the similarity is that the perspectives support the view that images of children are created by communities and differ based on culture, context and period of time.

Arthur et al. (2012, p. 20) suggest "the fact that children's lives differ in different cultures and in different centuries supports the view that images of children are created by communities". All of the perspectives recognise the rapid changes taking place in children's worlds and challenge dominant perspective. In practice the contemporary theories are employed in early childhood settings when educators find ways to work with children and families that (Arthur et al., 2012, p. 20):

- Engage in reflective practice, critical action and change
- Understand the importance of cultural contexts in children's learning
- Respect diversity and focus on equity and social justice
- Build effective partnerships with families, children and communities
- Enhance relationships and collaborative learning environments
- Focus on dispositions and processes of learning
- Provide meaningful curriculum that connects to children's social worlds and extends learning
- Engage in intentional teaching drawing on a repertoire of pedagogies
- Document children's learning in ways that acknowledge children's strengths and make children's thinking visible to children and staff.

Young children are therefore considered competent and capable who have many strengths. They are active actors within their contexts and actively work to understand the world in which they exist and, at the same time change the world through participation and interaction.

CHILDREN'S INVOLVEMENT IN THE RESEARCH PROCESS

Historically, children were viewed as objects to be studied and considered incompetent, unreliable and incomplete (Fargas-Malet, Dominic McSherry, Larkin, Robinson, 2010). The importance of children's involvement in the research process was not considered, providing a disempowered social position of children.

With contemporary perspectives about the childhood and childhood, so too have come new perspectives in children's involvement in the research process. For some traditional methods, this has included the adaption of traditional techniques such as observation and questionnaires (Punch, 2002), while there have been new developments of method such as the 'mosaic approach' (Clark & Moss, 2001) and narrative inquiry (Clandinin & Connelly, 1986). Punch (2002) identified three different approaches to research with children:

1. Children are viewed the same as adults and the approach employs the same methods as those used with them,
2. Children are viewed as completely different to adults and the approach uses ethnography (participant observation) to examine the children's world,
3. Children are viewed as similar to adults but with different levels of competencies. The approach has developed an array of innovative and adapted techniques.

Castelle (1990) stated that when the researcher listens to children as part of this enterprise, it acknowledges the human rights of children to actively participate in relevant social processes. As Cannella (1997, p. 10) agrees, "the most critical voices that are silent in our construction of early childhood education are the children with whom we work. Our constructions of research have not fostered methods that facilitate hearing that voice".

In recent years children have become more involved in the different stages of the research process, including the formation of research questions, planning, methodology, collecting data and analysing data (Coad & Evans, 2008). How a researcher views childhood will inform the choice of method, ethical practice, analysis and interpretation of the data (Christensen and Prout, 2002; Mayall, 2000; O'Kane, 2000; Punch, 2002).

There have been some attempts to increase the agentic potential of children in research (Chin, 2007; Kellett, 2010; Veale, 2005). Designing the research process to include children as active participants and collaborators recognises the inherent competence that children can offer (Blasi, 1996). Children may either become co-researchers or primary researchers. If young children become co-researchers, they are offered opportunities to make some (but not all) decisions about the research (Freeman & Mathison, 2009). If young children become primary researchers, they are in charge of identifying research questions, deciding on methods, collecting data, analysing data and reporting and disseminating the findings. The kind of research is seen as offering 'insider perspectives' from the child (Spyrou, 2011). As Kellett (2010, p. 105) argues:

Children observe with different eyes, ask different questions—they sometimes ask questions that adults do not even think of—have different concerns and immediate access to a peer culture where adults are outsiders. The research agendas children prioritize, the research questions they frame and the way in which they collect data are also quintessentially different from adults.

Though children's voice is sometimes presented as 'speaking for themselves', a form of analysis is always undertaken to allow an interpretation of what young children mean. For example, a reflexive approach to data analysis asks what kind of analytical frameworks the researcher imposes on children's voices. In some research with young children, often despite good intentions, researchers may simply fall back on their own adult semantic categories for analysis to make sense of what the child is telling them rather than having a clear understanding of the child's own semantics. Spyrou (2011) suggests that what children say means what the researchers understands rather than what the child means.

INFORMED CONSENT

Undertaking research with children takes place within a context of ethical practice and protection for the rights of the child. This approach is situated within the United Nations' Convention of the Rights of the Child in which it states:

Parties shall assure to the child who is capable of forming his or her own views the right to express those views freely in all matters affecting the child, the views of the child being given due weight in accordance with the age and maturity of the child. (Ibid, Article 12.1)

The child shall have the right to freedom of expression; this right shall include freedom to seek, receive and impart information and ideas of all kinds, regardless of frontiers, either orally, in writing or in print, in the form of art, or through any other media of the child's choice. (Ibid, Article 13.1)

Embodying these ethical articles requires the researcher to abide by the principles and ensure children's rights are respected and upheld.

Researchers must gain the co-operation from a range of gatekeepers (such as school staff and parents) when undertaking research with children (Cree et al., 2002). Informed consent should be freely given, without threat, persuasion or coercion by children who are able to make an informed decision. It has often been assumed that children are not competent enough to give their informed consent, and that is needs to be gained from a more competent adult (Kellet & Ding, 2004). Children are then positioned at a simpler level of agreement to participate or "assent" (Kellet & Ding, 2004, p. 166). However, competent young children can give their informed consent with competence defined as having enough knowledge to understand what is proposed and enough discretion to be able to make a wise decision in light of one's own interests (Alderson & Morrow, 2004). There are examples of where researchers have sought active consent from children and passive agreement from their guardians (Morrow, 2001; Thomas & O'Kane, 1998).

It is also argued that the notion of consent might exclude some children (such as disabled or refugee children) where informed consent may not be possible to obtain in particular contexts (Cocks, 2006). Cocks (2006, p. 257) argues that concept of 'assent' is sensitive and an appropriate option to include all children in research on issues that affect them, "removing the reliance on the child demonstrating adult-centric attributes such as maturity, competence and completeness". Children's assent can therefore be assessed by the researcher being attentive to the children's behaviour and response towards them at all times.

Information about projects and informed consent have been given as information leaflets, tapes, letters and oral presentations to children, their families and other gatekeepers (Barker & Weller, 2003; Morgan et al., 2002). The quality of the information provided within the materials is important as the ability to give informed consent depends on the quality of the explanations (Bogolub & Thomas, 2005). In printed material, this includes the use of simple language (short sentences, no jargon and the use of requests rather than demands). It has also found to be useful for information to be broken up into short sections, with subheadings. It is advisable to run through draft printed material with children and ask for their views (Alderson, 2004).

In a recent study Harcourt (2011) created a research partnership with young children before gaining informed consent. Within the context there were many discussion with the children over the roles and responsibilities of those participating in the research project in order to develop intersubjectivity (Rogoff, 1998). Once information about the project had been carefully considered by all of the potential research participants, discussion moved to documenting consent. Children in the early childhood service decided to write 'ok' as their signature for consent. The children also decided to write 'ok' each time they agreed to work with adults.

VOICE

The concept of 'children's voice' has received greater focus in child-centred research. Many studies have recognised the competence of children as informants (Christensen, 2004; Danby, 2002; Forrester, 2002). Recognising children as competent verbal and nonverbal communicators allows for new insights of how they construct their social worlds (Christensen & James, 2000; Danby, 2002). Spyrou (2011, p. 151) suggests that "one could argue that the interdisciplinary field of childhood studies has built its very *raison d'être* around the notion of children's voice. By accessing the otherwise silenced voices of children—by giving children a voice—and presenting them to the rest of the world, researchers hope to gain a better understanding of childhood". The concept of children's voice is further strengthened by a moral perspective when children's voice is considered to empower the social position of children and childhood from a social justice and rights perspective.

Researchers have explored different ways of eliciting children's experiences and voices that do not necessarily depend on interaction with an interviewer. Some of these methods include scenarios, vignettes and sentence completion tasks or methods which use technology (Greene & Hill, 2006). Other techniques include role play and drama (Christensen & James, 2000), the use of digital spaces where children might feel more comfortable (McWilliam et al., 2009) and the use of radio discussions (Young & Barrett, 2001).

In a study on children's view on starting school in Australia, Dockett and Perry (2003) remarked that including children in dialogue on their direct experiences had the potential to inform adults of the implications and outcomes of these experiences for young children themselves. By involving children in these open discussion, adults are coming to regard children as "competent and interpretive social participants" (2003, p. 12). Farrell et al. (2002, p. 28) states that listening to children is imperative as children's "own accounts give voice to their distinctive experience".

CONTEXT OF RESEARCH

With any research project, it is important to understand the importance of context and how this might influence what children talk about (Hill, 2006; O'Kane, 2000; Punch, 2002). When considering context it is important to consider privacy for the child and how to ensure a strong level of confidentiality. For example, some parents may tent to ask their child or the researcher about the interview of data collection. This process may place stress upon the child (Masson, 2004) or the researcher (Bushin, 2007). Confidentiality has been expressed by some researchers with phrases of "this is just between you and me" stated to the child at the commencement of the data collection (Thompson & Rudolph, 2000, p. 35).

A possible context for exploration could be the child's own home. Research collected from the child's home however may be more time-consuming and costly (Scott, 2000). In the child's home, the researcher needs to negotiate their social position as a guest (Mayall, 2000). Also, the parent or guardian may wish to be present in the data collection, which may influence the child's responses (Scott, 2000).

Another possible site for data collection is the school, however different problems have been identified regarding the school setting. These include:

• The setting of the school such as limitation of the timetable and difficulties in finding available space (Kellet & Ding, 2004).
• Even though the vast majority of children may agree to participate, a minority of children may just write and/or say barely anything (Morrow, 2001).
• Risk of children interpreting participation in the research project as 'school work' (Kellet & Ding, 2004).
• The role of the researcher perceived as a 'teacher' by the child (Hill, 2006).
• Children might say what they think adults want them to say (Clark, 2005).

Researchers have tried to minimize these risks by emphasising to young children that there is no right or wrong answer (Punch, 2002a). Certain rooms in the school may represent a suitable world for the child between the formal and informal worlds of the school. For example, the arts room (Darbyshire et al., 2005) or the storage cupboard (Jones, 2008) have found used by researchers as more of a neutral space. This is an important consideration when conducting research with young children in school settings.

DATA COLLECTION

Researchers may engage with children to explore their own voice. This process requires a level of rapport to be established. When establishing rapport with young children, it is recommended to start with a period of 'free narrative' when starting an interview to allow the child to settle into the setting and also to allow the research to grasp the child's communication style and concerns (Cameron, 2005). The researcher can also ask the child about things they already know that appear relatively unthreatening (Cameron, 2005) such as specific daily events, routines or feelings (Mauthner, 1997).

The role of the researcher in conversations with a child should also include suitable non-verbal behaviours (e.g., eye contact, head nods) and verbal prompts (e.g., 'tell me more')which indicate that the interviewer is listening and wants to hear the child's story (Cameron, 2005). Cameron (2005, p. 603) suggests phrases such as "great" or "cool" may not be suitable as they "may discourage the child from telling the whole story which includes the non-cool parts".

Researchers with young children are recommended to avoid using closed questions with young children and instead use a wide range of open ended questions (Waterman et al., 2001). An understanding of the child's interests and experiences is also important. Young children tend to give monosyllabic answers to questions they do not consider relevant to them (Morgan et al., 2002).

A wide range of activities and techniques have been used in interviews and focus groups with young children to make them more enjoyable and interesting and to also allow the child to take control of the focus and agenda (Kay et al., 2003; Sanders & Munford, 2005). Some researchers have used refreshment breaks (Morgan et al., 2002) or food breaks (Goodenough et al., 2003) to keep children engaged and focused, as well as allowing extra non-structured informal time. Using a mixture of materials and techniques during the interview process also allows young children time to think about what they would like to communicate so they do not feel pressured to give a rapid response (Punch, 2002b). The processes also give children choice and control over how to express themselves (Morgan et al., 2002). After an interview of focus group, it may also be appropriate to have some sort of debriefing (Clark, 2005).

In a recent study of Chinese school aged children, Morrison (2013) developed a list of ten strategies to help ease interview situations with children even when the interviewer did not speak the language of these children. These strategies included:

1. Good relations between educators and children and between parents and the school.
2. Interviewers used several deliberate tactics to put the children at ease (such as open ended questions, verbal and non-verbal positive reinforcement, and understanding that not all questions had to be answered)
3. The interviewer had deliberately dressed formal to send a message to the children that the research was important.
4. The research assistant was a native speaker of the children's language and had a friendly disposition.
5. At the start of the interview it was set out clearly how it would operate, creating an atmosphere of positive feedback to the students. The interviewer was also careful not to take children and was always aware of time.
6. The interviewers were careful about proxemics in two main ways: the use of physical space and the use of non-verbal communication.
7. Care was taken with the question structure, terminology use, the question wording and the sequence of the interview.
8. The interviewers made the interview situation very concrete.
9. The interviewers were acutely aware of, and looking out for, hesitancies, one-word or one-phase answers, silences and the nonverbal behaviour of children.
10. The interviewers were visible in the school throughout the year of the project, so that the children would see them outside the interview situation.

The strategies allowed the interviewer to operate in the child's frame of reference. The strategies and structure provided security to children by making what begins as a strange situation become as familiar as possible in the setting of the children's experiences.

THE USE OF NARRATIVES IN CONTEMPORARY TIMES

Children's experiences are organised in narrative form within the memory. Narrative is considered a 'universal mode of thought' and a 'form of thinking' (Bruner, 1986; Nelson, 1998, 2007). According to Haakarainen et al. (2013, p. 215), "from the cultural-historical perspective, a narrative could be defined as a psychological tool formalising and unifying human thought and knowledge into thematic units—units of thought". Accordingly, narrative is the smallest cell of human thinking, providing insight into the child's experiences. As Vygotsky described (1962, p. 126), "thought undergoes many changes as it turns into speech. It does not merely find expression in speech; it finds reality and form."

Narrative research in contemporary times can also free social scientists from the rhetorical forms (Emihovich, 1995) that alienate children and families from their own traditions. Through the use of narrative we are able to recognise the power of subjectivity in allowing open dialogue and co-construction of meaning. Becoming comfortable with narrative research also means accepting ideas that the world has no fixed rules for assigning behaviour (Emihovich, 1995). This means that open dialogue is required to build consensus around shared meaning and to ensure the inclusion of multiple voices. Thus as Bruner (1986, p. 144) notes, "narrative structures are not only structures of meaning but structures of power as well".

The use of narrative as a contemporary research technique allows young children to share their experiences with others. Bruner (1990) tells us that small children are interested in human interaction and activity, the temporal sequences and unexpected turns of events. Narrative descriptions exhibit human activity as purposeful engagement in the world (Polkinghorne, 1995). The research technique is respectful of the child's voice and allows the child to choose what they would like to share with others (participation). Contemporary research can choose many different approaches to collect narratives and analyse narratives that will be discussed in later chapters in this book. Greater awareness and understanding however is needed for the widespread importance of narrative as a sense-making form for young children (Bamberg, 2007; Bruner, 1990, 2002; van Oers, 2003). This book helps to fill this void, by providing detailed evidence of the importance of narratives when researching with young children. Narrative research is an important methodology that ultimately collects stories as well as creates stories. You will discover is a tool for data collection as well as data analysis. Chapter 2 provides an overview of narratives approaches, exploring the different rhetorics. In the rest of the book you will also learn more about ways of working with narrative approaches and young children. You will come to understand the importance of implementing narrative approaches in contemporary times to provide new meaning of children's lives.

VALIDITY OF NARRATIVES

Validity in narrative research refers to the "believability of a statement or knowledge claim" (Polkinghorne, 2007, p. 474). Thus, readers will judge the validity of our work as researchers, they are the people who must be convinced that a knowledge claim is justified. Differences emerge however based on people's viewpoints. It is for this reason traditional understandings of validity may not represent the postmodern world. Alternative notions of validity can be used such as trustworthiness (Lincoln & Guba, 1985),"verisimilitude" (Ellis & Bochner, 2000, p. 751), "truthlike observations" (Barone & Eisner, 1997, p. 74) and "crystallisation" (Richardson, 2000, p. 934). For example, Richardson's (2000) notion of "crystallization— deconstructs the traditional idea of 'validity'" by recognising that there are more than three sides (reliability, validity and generalisability) from which to view the world. Polkinghorne (2007) further suggests that in narrative research readers are asked "to make judgements on whether or not the evidence and argument convinces them at the level of plausibility, credibleness, or trustworthiness of the claim" (p. 477). Validity therefore relates to personal meaning drawn from the narrative stories, not to a measurable truth.

OUR STANCE

In the book we will show the importance of narrative and young children. The intention is to highlight a variety of ways narrative can be used as an analytical tool by educators and others working with young children. We believe narratives are an important contemporary approach for understanding young children and their understanding of the world. We also believe that narratives provide important insights into the cultural contexts in which children live.

All of the authors have come to know the importance of narrative with children during their PhD studies. The chosen methodology allowed the authors to create new understandings about children's understanding in contemporary times. From this experience we have become advocates for narratives approaches as contemporary ways to work with young children. We believe that narratives are able to extend our understanding about early childhood and provide new ways for exploring meaning. We also realise that there is much work yet to do with narrative research and young children, however this book allows others interested to come to know the current research field.

We also acknowledge that the narratives that young children tell may sometimes be fragmented and not linear. This is highly important for understanding the different structures of narratives and to acknowledge each narrative has a unique form and presentation. Children's narrative may be similar or different to an adult's conceptualisation of a narrative.

The chapters in this book will show how understanding narrative and young children also provide opportunities to explore themes of place, generation, gender, ethnicity, democracy, digital technology, ableness and sustainability. These themes are important for the daily lives of young children and those who work with young children. New insights are shared from children's perspectives that may otherwise have been left un-analysed in early childhood settings and schools.

CONCLUSION

Researchers conducting research with young children have developed and continue to adapt social research methods and tools to achieve the aims of their study with the characteristics and needs of young children. The new approaches allow new understanding of children's perspectives and experiences and provide greater insights into children's worlds and meaning-making. While they achieve greater empowerment for children, it is important however to consider that methods and techniques with young children still need to be reflexively and critically approached. As Punch (2002a, p. 33) questions, "are certain methods being used with children purely because they are fun, or because they also generate useful and relevant data?"

This chapter has provided an overview of current contemporary understanding of early childhood education and research. In the next chapter you will read of the importance of narrative as a method for research with young children. The chapter will provide details on the rhetoric of narrative and you will begin to explore the usefulness of narratives in modern times to understand knowledge and thinking. You will discover how the use of narrative as a contemporary research method empowers children to be heard and respected by adults. The approach also allows a sharing of understanding, knowledge and trust in the research approach. The new space for exploration allows narratives to be implemented by adults (including researchers and educators) to provide new ways to illuminate the children's experiences and to challenge what is considered 'normal' from an adult perspective.

REFERENCES

Alanen, L., Kiili, J., Kuukka, A., & Lehiten, A. R. (2005). *Health, wellbeing and children's agency.* In *GEMS of the health promotion research programme.* Tampere, Finland: Cancer Society of Finland and Academy of Finland.

Alderson, P. (2004). Ethics. In S. Fraser, V. Lewis, S. Ding, M. Kellet, & C. Robinson (Eds.), *Doing research with children and young people* (pp. 97–112). London: The Open University.

Alderson, P., & Morrow, V. (2004). *Ethics, social research and consulting with children and young people.* Essex: Barnado's.

Arthur, L., Beecher, B., Death, E., Dockett, S., & Farmer, S. (2012). *Programming and planning in early childhood settings.* Sydney: Cengage Learning.

Bamberg, M. G. W. (Ed.). (2007). *Narrative: State of the art.* Amsterdam: John Benjamins.

Barker, J., & Weller, S. (2003). Is it fun? Developing children centred research methods. *International Journal of Sociology and Social Policy, 23*(1/2), 33–58.

Barone, T., & Eisner, E. (1997), Arts-based educational research. In R. Jaeger (Ed.), *Complementary methods for research in education* (2nd ed., pp. 73–116). Washington, DC: American Educational Research Association.

Blasi, M. J. (1996). Pedagogy: Passivity or possibility. *Childhood Education, 72*(3), 130–132.

Bogolub, E. B., & Thomas, N. (2005). Parental consent and the ethics of research with foster children: beginning a cross-cultural dialogue. *Qualitative Social Work, 4*(3), 271–292.

Bruner, J. S. (1986). *Actual minds, possible worlds.* Cambridge, MA: Harvard University Press.

Bruner, J. S. (1990). *Acts of meaning.* Cambridge, MA: Harvard University Press.

Bruner, J. S. (2002). *Making stories: Law, literature, life.* Cambridge, MA: Harvard University Press.

Bushin, N. (2007). Interviewing with children in their homes: Putting ethical principles into practice an developing flexible techniques. *Children's Geographies, 5*(3), 235–251.

Buckingham, D. (2000). *After the death of childhood.* Cambridge: Polity Press in association with Blackwell Publishers.

Bourdieu, P. (1993). *Sociology in question.* London: Sage.

Cameron, H. (2005). Asking the tough questions: A guide to ethical practices in interviewing young children. *Early Childhood Development and Care, 175*(6), 597–610.

Canella, G. (1997). *Deconstructing early childhood education: Social justice and revolution.* New York, NY: Peter Lang.

Castelle, K. (1990). *In the child's best interest: A primer on the U.N. Convention on the Rights of the Child.* East Greenwich, RI: Plan International.

Chin, E. (2007). Power-puff ethnography/guerrilla research: Children as native anthropologists. In A. Best (Ed.), *Representing young: Methodological issues in critical youth studies* (pp. 269–283). New York, NY: New York University Press.

Christensen, P. (2004). Children's participation in ethnographic research: Issues of power and representation. *Children & Society, 18*, 165–176.

Christensen, P., & James, A. (2000). Childhood diversity and commonality. Some methodological insights. In P. Christensen & A. James (Eds.), *Research with children: Perspectives and practices* (pp. 160–178). London: Falmer Press.

Christensen, P., & Prout, A. (2002). Working with ethical symmetry in social research with children. *Children, 9*(4), 477–497.

Clark, A. (2005). Listening to and involving young children: A review of research and practice. *Early Child Development and Care, 175*(6), 489–505.

Clark, A., & Moss, P. (2001). *Listening to young children: The Mosaic approach.* London: National Children's Bureau.

Coad, J., & Evans, R. (2008). Reflections on practical approaches to involving children and young people in the data analysis process. *Children and Society, 22*(1), 41–52.

Cocks, A. J. (2006). The ethical maze: Finding an inclusive path towards gaining children's agreement to research participation. *Childhood, 13*(2), 247–266.

Cree, V. E., Kay, H., & Tisdall, R. (2002). Research with children: Sharing the dilemmas. *Childhood and Family Social Work, 7*, 47–56.

Curtis, D., & Carter, M. (2000). *The art of awareness: How observations can transform your teaching.* St Paul, MN: Redleaf Press.

Dahlberg, G., Moss, P., & Pence, A. (2007). *Beyond quality in early childhood education and care: Postmodern perspectives.* London: Falmer Press.

Danby, S. (2002). The communicative competence of young children. *Australian Journal of Early Childhood, 27*(3), 25–30.

Darbyshire, P., MacDougall, C., & Schiller, W. (2005). Multiple methods in qualitative research with children: More insight or just more? *Qualitative Research, 5*(4), 417–436.

Dockett, S., & Perry, B. (2003). Children's views and children's voices in starting school. *Australian Journal of Early Childhood, 28*(1), 12–17.

Ellis, C., & Bochner, A. (2000), Autoethnography, personal narrative, reflexivity. In N. Denzin & Y. Lincoln (Eds.), *Handbook of qualitative research* (2nd ed., pp. 733–768). Thousand Oaks, CA:Sage.

Emilhovich, C. (1995). Distancing passion: Narratives in social science. In J. A. Hatch & R. Wisniewski (Eds.), *Life histories and narrative* (pp. 37–48). London: Falmer Press.

Fargas-Malet, M., McSherry, D., Larkin, E., & Robinson, C. (2010). Research with children: Methodological issues and innovative techniques. *Journal of Early Childhood Research, 8*(2), 175–192.

Farrell, A., Tayler, C., Tennent, L., & Gahan, D. (2002). Listening to children: A study of child and family services. *Early Years, 22*(1), 27–38.

Forrester, M. (2002). Appropriating cultural conceptions of childhood: Participation in conversation. *Childhood, 9*(3), 255–276.

Foucault, M. (1978). *History of sexuality: An introduction.* London: Penguin.

Freeman, M. (1998). The sociology of childhood and children's rights. *International Journal of Children's Rights, 6*, 433–444.

Freeman, M., & Mathison, S. (2009). *Researching children's experiences.* New York, NY: The Guilford Press.

Goodenough, T., Williamson, E., Kent, J., & Ashcroft, R. (2003). "What did you think about that?" Researching children's perceptions of participation in a longitudinal genetic epidemiological study. *Children and Society, 17*, 113–125.

Greene, S., & Hogan, D. (Eds.). (2005). *Researching children's experience: Approaches and methods.* London: SAGE.

Grieshaber, S., & Cannella, G. (2001). From identity to identities: Increasing possibilities in early childhood education. In S. Grieshaber & G. Cannella (Eds.), *Embracing identities in early childhood education: Diversity and possibilities.* New York, NY: Teachers College Press.

Gutierrez, K. D., Larson, J., Enciso, P., & Ryan, C. (2007). Discussing expanded spaces for learning. *Languages Arts, 85*(1), 69–77.

Hakkarainen, P., Brėdikytė, M., Jakkula, K., & Munter, H. (2013). Adult play guidance and children's play development in a narrative play-world. *European Early Childhood Education Research Journal, 21*(2), 213–225.

Harcourt, D. (2011). An encounter with children: seeking meaning and understanding about childhood. *European Early Childhood Education Research Journal, 19*(3), 331–343.

Hill, M. (2006). Children's voices on ways of having a voice: Children's and young people's perspectives on methods used in research and consultation. *Childhood, 13*(1), 69–83.

Hilton, M. (1996). Introduction: The children of this world. In M. Hilton (Ed.), *Potential fictions: Children's literacy and the challenge of popular culture.* London: Routledge.

James, A., Jenks, C., & Prout, A. (1998). *Theorising Childhood.* Cambridge, MA: Polity Press.

Jipson, J. (2001). Resistance and representation: Rethinking childhood education. In J. Jipson & R. Johnson (Eds.), *Resistance and representation: Rethinking childhood education.* New York, NY: Peter Lang.

Jones, K. (2008). It's well good sitting in the store cupboard just talking about what we do: Considering the spaces/places of research within children's geographies. *Children's Geographies, 6*(3), 327–332.

Jones Diaz, C., Beecher, B., & Arthur, L. (2007). Children's worlds: Globalisation and critical literacy. In L. Makin, C. Jones Diaz, & C Mclachlan (Eds.), *Literacies in childhood.* Sydney: Elsevier.

Kay, H., Cress, V., Tisdall, K., & Wallace, J. (2003). At the edge: negotiating boundaries in research with children and young people. *Forum: Qualitative Social Research, 4*(2).

Kellett, M. (2010). *Rethinking children and research: Attitudes in contemporary society.* London: Continuum.

Kellett, M., & Ding, S. (2004). Middle childhood. In S. Fraser, V. Lewis, S. Ding, M. Kellet, & C. Robinsons (Eds.), *Doing research with children and young people* (pp. 161–174). London: The Open University.

Kenway, J., & Bullen, E. (2001). *Consuming children: Education-entertainment-advertising.* Buckingham: Open University Press.

Lehtinen, A. (2004). *Children as agents—the core elements of agency.* Unpublished manuscript, Jyvaskyla, Finland.

Lewis, A. (2002). Accessing through research interviews the views of children with difficulties in learning. *Support for Learning, 17*(3), 110–116.

Lincoln, Y., & Guba, E. (1985). *Naturalistic inquiry.* Beverly Hill, CA: Sage.

MacNaughton, G. (1995). A post-structuralist analysis of learning in early childhood settings. In M. Fleer (Ed.), *DAPcentrism: Challenging developmentally appropriate practice.* Canberra: Australian Early Childhood Association.

MacNaughton, G. (2003). *Shaping early childhood: Learners, curriculums and contexts*. Maidenhead: Open University Press.

Malaguzzi, L. (1998). History, ideas and basic philosophy. In C. Edwards, L. Gandini, & G. Foreman (Eds.), *The hundred languages of children*. Norwood, NJ: Ablex.

Masson, J. (2004). The legal context. In S. Fraser, V. Lewis, S. Ding, M. Kellet, & C. Robinson (Eds.), *Doing research with children and young people* (pp. 43–58). London: The Open University.

Mauthner, M. (1997). Methodological aspects of collecting data from children: Lessons from three research projects. *Children and Society, 11*, 16–28.

Mayall, B. (2000). Conversations with children. Working with generational issues. In P. Christensen & A. James (Eds.), *Research with children: Perspectives and practices* (pp. 120–135). London: Falmer Press.

Mayall, B. (2002). *Towards a sociology for childhood: Thinking from children's lives*. Buckingham: Open University Press.

McWilliam, E., Dooley, K., McArdle, R., & Pei-Ling Tan, J. (2009). Voicing objections. In A. Jackson & L. Mazzei (Eds.), *Voice in qualitative inquiry: Challenging conventional, interpretative, and critical conception in qualitative research* (pp. 63–75). London: Routledge.

Moll, L., Amanti, C., Neff, D., & Gonzalez, N. (1992). Funds of knowledge for teaching: Using a qualitative approach to connect homes and classrooms. *Theory into Practice, 31*(2), 132–141.

Morgan, M., Gibbs, S., Maxwell, K., & Britten, N. (2002). Hearing children's voices: Methodological issues in conducting focus groups with children aged 7–11 years. *Qualitative Research, 2*(5), 5–20.

Morrison, K. (2013). Interviewing children in uncomfortable settings: 10 lessons for effective practice. *Educational Studies, 39*(3), 320–337.

Morrow, V. (2001). Using qualitative methods to elicit young people's perspectives on their environments: Some ideas for community health initiatives. *Health Education Research: Theory and Practice, 16*(3), 255–268.

Nelson, K. (1998). *Language in cognitive development*. New York, NY: Cambridge University Press.

Nelson, K. (2007). *Young minds in social worlds: Experience, meaning, and memory*. Cambridge, MA: Harvard University Press.

O'Kane, C. (2000). The development or participatory techniques. Facilitating children's views about decisions which affect them. In P. Christensen & A. James (Eds.), *Research with children: Perspectives and practices* (pp. 120–135). London: Falmer Press.

Polkinghorne, D. E. (1995). Narrative configuration in qualitative analysis. In J. A. Hatch & R. Wisniewski (Eds.), *Life histories and narrative* (pp. 5–24). London: Falmer Press.

Polkinghorne, D. (2007), Validity issues in narrative research. *Qualitative Inquiry, 13*(4), 471–486.

Prout, A. (2003). Participation, policy and childhood. In C. Hallett & A. Prout (Eds.), *Hearing the voices of children: Social policy for a new century*. London: Routledge Falmer.

Punch, S. (2002a). Research with children: the same or different from research with adults? *Childhood, 9*(3), 321–341.

Punch, S. (2002b). Interviewing strategies with young people: The "secret box", stimulus material and task-based activities. *Children and Society, 16*, 45–56.

Richardson, L. (2000), Writing: A method of inquiry. In N. Denzin & Y. Lincoln (Eds.), *Handbook of qualitative research* (2nd ed., pp. 923–948). Thousand Oaks, CA: Sage.

Rogoff, B. (1998). Cognition as a collaborative process. In W. Damon, D. Kuhn, & R. S Siegler (Eds.), *Cognitive, perceptions and language* (5th ed., pp. 679–744). New York, NY: John Wiley and Sons Inc.

Rogoff, B. (2003). *The cultural nature of human development*. Oxford: Oxford University Press.

Sanders, J., & Munford, R. (2005). Activity and reflection: research and change with diverse groups of young people. *Qualitative Social Work, 4*(2), 197–209.

Scott, J. (2000). Children as respondents. The challenge for quantitative methods. In P. Christensen & A. James (Eds.), *Research with children: Perspectives and practices* (pp. 98–119). London: Routledge Falmer.

Spyrou, S. (2011). The limits of children's voices: From authenticity to critical, reflexive representation. *Childhood, 18*(2), 151–165.

Thomas, N., & O'Kane, C. (1998). The ethics of participatory research with children. *Children and Society, 12*, 336–348.

Thompson, C., & Rudolph, L. (2000). *Counseling children*. Belmont, CA: Wadsworth Brooks/Cole.

United Nations. (1989). *Convention on the rights of the child*. Geneva: United Nations.

van Oers, B. (Ed.). (2003). *Narratives of childhood: Theoretical and practical explorations for the innovation of early childhood education*. Amsterdam: VU University Press.

Veale, A. (2005). Creative methodologies in participatory research with children. In S. Greene & D. Hogan (Eds.), *Researching children's experience: Approaches and methods* (pp. 253–272). London: SAGE.

Vygotsky, L. (1978). *Mind in society: The development of higher psychological processes*. Cambridge, MA: Harvard University Press.

Waterman, A. H., Blades, M., & Spencer, C. (2001). Interviewing children and adults: The effect of question format on the tendency to speculate. *Applied Cognitive Psychology, 15*(3), 301–320.

Woodrow, C., & Brennan, M. (2001). Interrupting dominant images: Critical and ethical issues. In J. Jipson & R. Johnson (Eds.), *Resistance and representation: Rethinking childhood education* (pp. 1–8). New York, NY: Peter Lang

Young, L., & Barrett, H. (2001). Issues of access and identity: Adapting research methods with Kampala street children. *Childhood, 8*(3), 383–395.

Susanne Garvis
University of Gothenburg

TRADITIONS AND TURNS—PATHWAYS IN NARRATIVE METHODOLOGY

INTRODUCTION

As pointed out by numerous researchers within the human and social sciences, narrative is ever present in human lives and a common mode of communication. For those reasons narrative genres has been found productive across a range of disciplines and in research fields like education, as well as in child, culture and society studies. Narrative methodology offers a range of ways for understanding children, their lives and what conditions them and illuminates children's meaning-making, their activities and experiences. The consequence of such a methodology will hopefully be that children are valued as human beings in their own right and are approached in research as participants one way or another.

In the process of developing an appropriate narrative design, the advantage of taking informed routes and choices is obvious. The student researcher that finds narrative designs appealing and appreciates the rich potential sources for new knowledge and insights will easily, as a paradox, be more uncertain as the reading escalates. For the more experienced researcher, the number of different narrative designs can cause confusion and ambiguity in the process of designing a research project. In the practice of becoming a skilled researcher in narrative methodology, a number of diverse approaches are revealed and association with traditions and connections to earlier research are made. As researchers we easily find ourselves traversing borderlands and navigating from one paradigm to another (Clandinin & Rosiek, 2007). As narrative inquiry indeed is still a field in making (Chase, 2011), new pathways can be made as this book attempts to, by exploring narrative methodology designed to meet the contemporary research of children's lives and stories in early childhood education.

This chapter will provide the reader with background knowledge on some relevant traditions in narrative research and hence new pathways and narrative designs can be developed. The field is too wide and complex for a complete genealogy mapping of all pathways and borderlands, divergences and newness in one chapter. Therefore the historical emergence will first only briefly be sketched. Turns, divergences and varieties will be discussed. We will see that what counts as stories varies, as do what kinds of stories have been studied and how the researcher designs the study.

Within the framework of narrative research, researchers have used different approaches, strategies and methods to collect or produce stories. Some narrative methodologies follow the traditions of language studies, while others follow psychological, developmental, anthropological, sociological and educational studies of didactics. The reader is encouraged to reflect on these different pathways in narrative methodology and critically relate to them in their own design and research processes.

In this chapter a distinction is made between *narrative,* meaning both a story and its telling, the process of constructing story. *Narrative methodology* will refer to research in the scientific landscape where narrative is used in ways that differ (e.g., as the products of anthropology and case studies, and in methods of ethnography and interviews). *Narrative analysis* will mean an approach where the researcher narrates based on data. Since analysis always will be the researcher's construct, this will include *analysis of narrative*, which is a certain approach, where the researcher analyses stories (Polkinghorne, 1995). *Narrative inquiry* here will refer to a method of investigation into a problem, following pragmatism, inspired by John Dewey (1934). Following this tradition, narrative inquiry will also mean a way of knowing by telling and reflecting. "Narrative inquiry is a way of understanding experience. It is collaboration between researchers and participants, over time in a place or series of places, and in social interaction with milieus" (Clandinin & Connelly, 2000, p. 20). We would add to this quote that in efforts to understand children, their teachers and the teachers for early childhood teachers we need to manoeuvre to and fro researching the individual stories and the macro social stories. Our position in contemporary research, as we will elaborate throughout this book, is that we are widely inspired by narrative traditions. As we will see throughout the book, we view children's personal narrative as co-constructs situated and belonging to a larger community, both on a personal as well as a discursive level. This book presents many examples where some form of polyphonic representation unfolds (Craigh, 2007; Garvis & Dwyer, 2013), which gives us a critical, pragmatic and a poststructural touch.

NARRATIVE METHODOLOGY—A BLURRED LANDSCAPE

Certain traditions belong to and have origin in a certain kind of research paradigm, which come with a suggested methodological approach and underpinning philosophy, therefore it could be useful to look for distinction and differences, as well as shared commitments. Traditions and their borderlands are, however, never clean cut and completely clear—the borders are rather blurred, traditions overlap and come together. Recent narrative methodology does not come from a singular continuous tradition, nor do the turns follow a one-way path, therefore the attempt here is rather to construct clusters of traditions and developments and turns, marked by familiarities and point to some borderlands.

Science is not necessarily cumulative, meaning that science does not follow a linear development, as pointed out by Kuhn in *The structure of scientific revolutions* (1970). He argued that what is considered scientific knowledge is dependent on human motivation and knowledge rather developing as paradigmatic shifts in three stages. Questions, problems and vague understandings are considered to be "pre-science", science without paradigmatic theories and connected methodology. Researchers motivated to solve problems and searching for new understandings can cause paradigmatic shifts if they are successful. "Normal science" can be productive to researchers following the paradigm. Kuhn's scientific view is not instrumentalist as he sees theories as tools for disclosing the world through their own conceptual articulation in the reflexive practice of research. His thoughts are relevant for this chapter as we can, through his guidance, view narrative research as a source for more than a personal single anecdote and more than historical chronology.

Understanding children is, for us, about understanding how the socio-cultural world shapes conditions for children's stories and narrative constructs in meaning-making and in shaping identities, in activities like play and learning. New knowledge of children belongs to the awareness of both the personal experience and the contextual relationships. How we understand the interconnectedness (or not) is all about concepts of human practice and how practice go hand-in-hand with bodily, visual or oral language, how the articulation belongs to scientific communities that uses one or assembled languages.

Let us illustrate the blurry landscape with a classical case study of children's oral narratives: Katherine Nelson's *Narratives from the Crib* (Nelson, 1989b). A variety of studies were conducted on an empirical base made from transcripts from audio recordings of bedtime conversations between 2-year-old Emily and her parents and Emily's pre-sleep monologues. The empirical data were collected over a period of 15 months. This collection of studies is organised in three paths, all from data of one talkative child:

1. *Constructing a world.* The study shows that a child represents real-life experiences and that her monologues can be seen as re-creation of her experiences. The cultural analysis is conducted by Katherine Nelson (Nelson, 1989b) and by Jerome Bruner and Joan Lucariello (Bruner & Lucariello, 1989). Carol Fleisher Feldman (1989) shows how Emily uses the narrative monologues to solve problems in her recent life experience.
2. *Constructing a language.* The study demonstrates how Emily's language develops and how this is done through monologues and dialogues. We learn that a child's monologues can be studied as a speech genre by the work of Julie Gerhardt (Gerhardt, 1989), and that the child uses what John Dore conceptualizes as *re-envoicement* (Dore, 1989) when she takes up words and sentences from her parents' talk. This is a concept inspired by Mikhail Bakhtin (Bakhtin, 1986).
3. *Constructing a self.* Rita Watson's study shows how a child regulates herself by monologues and participating in dialogues (Watson, 1989). Nelson reveals how Emily's narratives are a linguistic construction of self in time (Nelson, 1989a). Daniel Stern approaches the crib monologues from a psychoanalytic perspective, illuminating how a child at the age of around 15–18 months begins to construct a "verbal" sense of self and later how the narrative self emerges (Stern, 1989).

19

What we can learn by the case study of Emily's talk, is that it becomes obvious that Emily early in life represents events in which she participates, and we are offered detailed information about how the narrative language emerges and develops over time and how this is entwined with her life experiences and her dialogues with her parents. To make sense of the world Emily narrates important happenings—happenings that have taken place, which may take place and of uttermost important to Emily, what should take place. We learn that Emily's monologist narratives are not individual narratives, but rather socially and relationally conditioned. The study weaves together thematic analysis, content analysis, and structural analysis with relational analysis. Psychoanalytical perspectives here are related to socio-linguistic analysis.

From this classical example, together with a range of new research contributions, we can also learn that the ability to understand narrative emerges at a young age, and that the art of narration might be a predisposition to construct mental stories, but first of all that children learn and develop narrative structure through participating in a culture (Bruner, Feldman, Hermansen, & Molin, 2006; Wells, 1987).

The discourse of children being a participant in research, as we referred to in Chapter 1, is more common in contemporary research than when this classic research was conducted. Such ethical issues are addressed in the new edition of this book. In a foreword to the new edition, Emily Oster, the child being exposed in the studies, writes about the remembering of a recorder at the age of two, being observed and being exposed through analysis. Emily at age 25 writes that she has always known that there is a book about her. As she grew older, she paid more attention to what the book told her about her parents, then about herself. Furthermore she says:

> People sometimes ask me whether I plan to tape my own children, if they talk to themselves. I suppose I am still not sure. I love to read about what I was thinking as a toddler, but will my own children feel the same way, or might they prefer to talk to themselves alone? At the very least, just as my mother did, I plan to ask first. (Nelson, 2006, p. vii)

In our attempt to organise different narrative research traditions, we are, of course, not objective and write from contemporary issues and knowledge available at a certain time in research history. As researchers and authors, our approach is coloured by working in the landscape we are mapping. Our map is a construct where we aim to sketch out narrative methodology with relevance to the participants in the early childhood educational field. We will locate research in this field as we know it and as we find it productive for normative reasons, narrative methodology will help researchers in describing educational experiences from the perspectives of the agents there.

ORIGINS

The story of origin to the analysis of narratives varies in the methodologies literature. Some begin with the hermeneutic studies of religious texts like the Bible, the Talmud and the Koran, others start with studies of the antique Greek myths and philosophical anecdotes. In modern times, it is possible to point to the Russian formalist Vladimir Propp to set a starting point. In 1928 he published his *Morphology of the Folktale*, in which he analysed the underlying structures of the Russian folktales, also called the "wonder fairy tales". Postformalists such as Mikhail Bakhtin continued to develop narrative analysis from this source among others in Russia. After the Russian revolution in 1917 the East-West cooperation ceased for decades. Both of them were first translated into English and French in the 1960s and even later to other languages.

Eastern European traditions continued to be developed in the west by intellectual immigrants like the linguist Roman Jacobson and the literature theorist Tzvetan Todorov. This literary source of narrative studies was developed as contrary to traditional hermeneutics. It was the text as such that was of interest to the researcher, not the author's intentions or the circumstances of the text production (Czarniawska, 2004; Polkinghorne, 1988). New methodology was developed, for example Gadamer's hermeneutics. Such a critic is what Wolfgang Iser opposed when emphasising the relationship between the reader and the text. Propp's formalist analysis was taken up in the 1970s by William Labov and Joshua Waletzky. They suggested that sociolinguistics could be studied by syntagmatic analysis and argued that this would lead to understandings of simple as well as complex narratives (Labov & Waletzky, 2006).

The interest in narrative research spread rapidly beyond literature theory into the humanities and social sciences. Catherin Kohler Riessman traced the narrative turn to the United States and to *Chicago School of Sociology* where a group of researchers studied letters from Polish farmers and immigrants, urban boys and deviant groups from the beginning of last century. The Chicago school was central to the development of narrative research in anthropology, ethnographical writings (Atkinson, 2001; Riessman, 2008). Studies of communities, social, political and economic aspects of everyday life as well as social relationships were written as narrative analysis. For instance William Whyte in USA wrote the classic *Street Corner Society*, a narrative analysis that gave descriptions of criminal life spans in 1930s. Later came the critics of beliefs in narrative truth and the argument that narratives are constructed and anthropologists are authors. Clifford Geertz strengthens this argument in *Works and Lives: The anthropologist as author* (1988). The historical realism used narrative descriptions to situate the narrative in a certain context. Pierre Bourdieu has criticised claims that the researcher can narrate a self-biographical story as a narrative truth. He claims that self-narratives can construct illusions and strengthen conventions (Bourdieu & Wacquant, 1992; Grenfell, 2008; Stenensen, 2007).

At a general level these recognitions illustrate some of the turns in research in which narrative methodology is a part. Stefinee Pinnegar and J. Gary Daynes suggests four historical thematic turns in research that can be seen located in narrative inquiry (Pinnegar & Daynes, 2007):

1. The attention to relationships among the researcher and the researched,
2. the move from the use of number as the only relevant data source to the acceptance of words and language as data,

3. a change from a focus on the general and universal towards an interest of the local and the particular, and
4. the recognition of blurred genres of knowing

Positivist methodology is designed in beliefs that research is about finding certain truths. Consequently there will be concerns about reliability, about how to conduct the research appropriate. Focus will be on numbers and what they tell us. The researcher is not important, rather a sign of solid research is that the same result can be found if a new researcher can duplicate the design. The importance of the author of the research becomes an issue in postpositivist paradigms, as well as cultural studies and poststructuralism. This issue is well elaborated in *Writing Culture* (Clifford & Marcus, 1986). Jerome Bruner (2006) has referred to the differences of rationale between a *paradigmatic* and a *narrative* way of knowing. While the latter is a common way of capture a great variety of local practices and experiences, the former refers to a form of knowing that can bring overviews and statistical knowledge. The move towards narrative methodology is a turn from paradigmatic way of knowing towards narrative knowing.

Donald Polkinghorne points out that the term *narrative* has been employed by qualitative researchers with a variety of meanings. In the context of narrative inquiry, *narrative* refers to a language form in which events and happenings are organized into a temporal unity by means of a plot. He refers to Bruner's two types of cognition (1985). On the one hand is the paradigmatic, in which the researcher will search for resemblance as members of a category. On the other hand is the narrative, in which the researcher will shape a story by combining elements into a story that includes a plot. Polkinghorne argues that narrative inquiries are divided into these two distinct groups. The first one is *analysis of narratives*. The other is a *narrative analysis* (Polkinghorne, 1988, 1995). We notice that Polkinghorne makes a clear demarcation. As we shall see some researchers mix these and new narrative methodology will point to the blurred borderlines between these and other traditions.

Jean Clandinin & Jerry Rosiek explore a conceptual border between narrative inquiry following Dewey's theory of experience and three other philosophical traditions that all occasionally will use stories in one way or another. These are postpositivist research, critical theory following Marxist ideas and poststructuralism. All four traditions have shared commitments and operate in a landscape of borders.

Critical realism. A postpositivist methodology will operationally seek to produce data that can be observed. The idea is that something is real if can be observed. An effort will be made to search for a reality that we all share. Stories will be collecting in such designs in order to identify common themes and universal narrative structure. The narrative data does not reveal a personal continuing story, but the data are treated as fixed, often decontextualized.

Critical theory will strive for methods that can help people develop a more robust sense of reality and seek to analyse false consciousness. The philosophical roots could be traced back to Marxist philosophy. The individual perspective is not considered as valid, rather the important perspectives will be the macro-social story—how the material social life conditions the lives and thinking of humans. In analysis critical methodology will see experience as closely connected to ideologies.

Poststructuralism focuses on the linguistic and narrative structure of knowledge through opposing the idea that there is such a thing as one-to-one correspondence between a word and its object. On the contrary, a word will have normative binaries built-in before a study starts. Words hold relatively stable meanings because they are embedded in a larger system of social discourses. Following this tradition, individual story will be related to a broader context. Social discourses are seen as conditioning and shaping the individual's story of experience.

Pragmatism begins with the ontology of experience following Dewey. In this tradition the researcher focuses on the way the relational, the temporal and the continuous features of experience manifest in narrative form. The foci point is the living narrative experience. The researcher takes into consideration that narrative unfolds over time. Therefore events are connected, each event has a past, a present as it appears and an implied future. Doing narrative inquiry following this tradition, the inquiry is not transcendental, rather it is transactional meaning relational and social.

We have described and given some examples of how traditions align and misalign. Differences between these four traditions is shown by different focus and belief in the personal story (from reality or fiction) and how much on focus is given the social discourse. It also follows a line of difference between following a temporal continuous and coherent line in presenting data or allowing disconnected and contrasting stories to be presented beyond narrative coherence (Hyvarinen, Hyden, & Saarenheimo, 2010). At last we can see difference between traditions when it comes to what degree a personal story is co-narrated. Some researchers will strive for coherence, they might also add complexity. Others will challenge canonical stories and lives by telling highly surprising, contradictory and possible stories.

According to Clandinin and Rosiek, borders between traditions must be seen as borders on a map, they are only clear demarcations on the map, and they can be seen as abstractions. Following one tradition the researcher easily bumps up against another tradition. Rather than mark the territory in a design too clearly, a narrative research project could work on selected concepts and elaborate on what they will mean and how they will be used in the analysis. Kinships and relations to the blurred landscape of traditions can be notified. This is also supported by Barbara Czarniawska who states:

> Rather than striving for a rigorous narrative analysis or for purity of a genre, reading and writing of narratives will remain a creative activity, based on bisociations[1] and hybridizing. (Czarniawska, 2004, p. 664)

Despite the philosophical origin of narrative approaches, the central point is that researchers discuss people's lives in ways that represents them. In the following, we follow and develop the thread of children's interests and of contemporary early childhood education.

APPROACHES TO NARRATIVE METHODOLOGY

Following the model of Aristotle, the sequential, chronological and completeness in narratives are central. This model encourages cracks to be hidden from the writing. As the editors of a recent book in the series *Studies in Narrative, Beyond Narrative Coherence* (Hyvarinen, Hyden, & Saarenheimo, 2010) point out, meaning is made in a social context and the researcher is an agent that can strive to create coherence or decline coherence in the writing. Incoherent narratives, however, can present more challenging cases. This is in line with Jerome Bruner's distinction between scripts and narrative (Bruner, 1990) and his claim that it is "only when constituent beliefs in folk psychology are violated that narratives are constructed" (1990, p. 40).

The vitality of narrative research can, as earlier stated, play an important role in understanding complex issues like everyday life experiences in early childhood institutions. Complexity points to the necessity for a spectrum of narrative approaches following different philosophical and disciplinary traditions and fields in order to understand contemporary lives. A narrative approach can be appropriate if the research interest lies in understanding children in institutional life on a general level by making cases. For political or cultural reasons this can also be done from a certain perspective or motivated from the urge to shed light on a special area where the public have low level of insight and knowledge. Narrative approach can give voice to those often invisible, as children in general and special groups of children. Furthermore the approach can create new insights, reveal surprises and build new innovative models of thinking and understandings of early childhood education. The sector is in need for continuously inquiring how, for example, play, development, learning, equity, law, pedagogy, didactics, curriculum, belonging to families, communities and places differ and unfolded in local settings. Narrative approach can also create insight into unknown or vague phenomenon, routine or events where children take a part. A narrative design can also be appropriate for contextualising children's experiences and conditions for living their life, shaping identities and build knowledge about themselves, others and the world in an educational setting. That means that children's personal experiences can be nested to one another in a kaleidoscope of stories (Craig, 2007). In this way children can be part of historical, cultural issues, media, health, global sustainability and political knowledge.

Stories about children, events and cases where children take a part as well as children's stories are data for narrative analysis. While stories *about* children can be studied by interviewing, analysis of text or/and visual or sound material, analysis and participant observation, *children's stories and culture* can also be elicited by an approach where the researcher participates in children's creative activities like writing, drawing, photo stories, children initiated role playing and structured or led drama play. Spending time with children in participant observation will often be appropriate whether the researcher follows characteristics of critical realism, critical theory, poststructuralism or pragmatism.

Data can be treated as belonging to a respondent's subject, where the aim is to write up a certain person's story, perspective on certain events or phenomenon or voice. Data can also be treated as co-constructed by the respondent and the researcher and further narrated by the researcher. When narrative research follows the traces of structuralism, narrative analysis will deal with a spoken or written text where the researcher's task is to present an account of an event or series of events, chronologically connected. Often then narrative will be defined as a semiotic representation of a series of events meaningfully connected in a temporal and causal way. Meaning, however, will always be a result from the interaction between the reader and the text and cannot be reduced to temporality and causality (Herman & Vervaeck, 2001, p. 13).

Following a postclassical perspective, narrative analyses is presented as a process where stories are seen as a co-construction and put together by the researcher. Barbara Czarniawska is close to a poststructural edge when she suggests such a way to go about narrative analysis. In a field of practice, as early childhood educations are, the researcher can create designs where you watch how stories are made, collect, elicit or provoke them. Later you study what the stories tell you (interpretation), then how the stories are told (analysis). The next step is to unmake them (deconstruct the stories). The researcher then writes up a narrative analysis as the researcher's story. The researcher constructs a narrative following the logic of communication, telling a different story, underlining some crucial points, shaping cases to raise questions or be critical and so on. Validity could be strengthened by linking the researcher's construct to more research in the field in question (Czarniawska, 2004, p. 652).

ANALYSING CRITICAL EVENTS

Within stories of experience there are identified critical incidents, considered plots of events. A critical event approach to narrative includes documentation over time. Following this approach to narrative data provides researchers with a broad view and allows change of experience (Webster & Mertova, 2007a). Specific events trigger our memory and how we recall events. In designs for analysing children's stories and teacher's stories about children it must therefore be taken into consideration how children as teachers might remember more, and therefore tell more by communicating with others. The story told is not just a container for the experience, but it also shapes how we will continue to remember the event. Memories provide material for story telling and narrative consolidates memory and makes it possible to communicate and negotiate meaning with others (Pramling & Ødegaard, 2014). To tell about what happened must be seen as an active and creative memory act that can sustain or change through the co- and retelling process.

In such a narrative approach Leonard Webster and Patricie Mortova suggest that the researcher establish a time frame and location of the event being investigated and propose some possible questions for the researcher (Webster & Mertova,

25

Table 1. Analytical approaches to narrative analysis

Analytic approach	Paradigm	Key features	Narrative knowledge
Critical events	Socio-psychoanalytic, Pragmatic, Critical theory	Gather actual incidents and stories about children, interview, observation, text analysis, identification of themes, composing of cases	Personal teacher knowledge, development of professionalism and ethics, empowerment
Ethnographic narrative	Pedagogical anthropology, auto-ethnography, phenomenological, poststructural, critical theory	Participant observation, interviews, accounts, biographical writings, Composing narratives and cases	Researchers reflexivity, descriptive and detailed personal, situated and contextual knowledge, cultural formation, children's culture, empowerment etc.
Narrative play	Pedagogical anthropology, socio-cultural, phenomenological, poststructural	Participant observation, video-observation, children's responses on video-observation, Composing narratives and cases	Descriptive knowledge on identity, meaning-making, learning, exploration, cultural formation, children's culture, etc.
Socio-linguistic narratives	Pedagogical anthropology, Socio-cultural	Video-observation, audio-observation, Identifying learning processes and conditions	Descriptive and contextual knowledge on language learning and meaning-making, conditions for learning language
Dialogic narrative	Dialogism, socio-cultural	Video-observation, Identifying dialogical processes and relational conditions, identifying chronotopes and intertextuality	Descriptive knowledge about connections, coherence, context, conditions for participation, play, learning, teaching, political, historical, cultural disclosure

2007, p. 86). Following these we propose some adjustments to the questions to invite children to tell about a critical event:

- Think of one memory you have on [context of investigation]. Can you tell me about it?
- Thinking back to [context of investigation], what do you remember or recall?
- What is it that you remember the most from [context of investigation]?
- Do you remember something from the [context of investigation]that scared you, made you angry or joyful?
- What do you think happened to you? How do you feel about what happened?
- What did your friends/parents/teachers do when this happened?
- Would you like to draw it?
- What is the drawing about? Where are you? What happened to you? Where are the others?

Informal communication adds opportunities to provide research data. The story teller communicates the level of criticality when telling stories to the researcher and informal opportunities can be an opportunity to validate data. In the process of analysis the researcher must be aware that critical events are not necessarily told as such. A critical event could be communicated in vague and implicit ways. When identifying critical event narratives, the researcher can look for marks and signs within a specific community context like:

- events that have had an impact on the people involved
- have had life-changing consequences
- are unplanned
- may reveal patterns of coherence
- are identified after the event
- are personal with strong emotional involvement

Critical event narrative proved to be a very viable and productive tool for staff development in early childhood institutions, teacher training practice and in the work of newly qualified teachers in Scandinavia. In this work, both written and oral narratives about children have been a tool for professional reasons and for researching such processes (Birkeland, 1998, 2007; Ødegaard & Birkeland, 2002; Ødegaard & Økland, 2015). The identification of *blunder stories* where the turning point is emphasized, brought forth self-reflection with a potential to change practice. Blunder stories were identified in communities of practice characterized by reciprocal thrust and humorous atmospheres (Birkeland, 2007; Ødegaard & Birkeland, 2002). The Scandinavian experiences are associated with frequent references to the pragmatic tradition of teachers' stories of identity and professional development (Clandinin & Connelly, 2000; Webster & Mertova, 2007b; Wilson & Ritchie, 2000).

ANALYSIS AS ETHNOGRAPHIC NARRATIVE

Ethnographic design is an established approach within classroom studies and the studies of early childhood education, which can be labelled pedagogical anthropology (Gulløv, Anderson, & Valentin, 2010). Such narrative research provides rich descriptions of teacher practices and children's experiences often presented as case studies. However, explicit references to the process of research, the analysis of the empirical data on which findings and the new knowledge are based, have until now been insubstantial. A mapping of Scandinavian early childhood educational research for the years 2006–2007–2008 shows that pedagogical ethnography is a popular design, but that a huge range of published articles within the early childhood field contained little information about analytic and methodological issues (Nordenbo & Moser, 2009).

Pedagogical research studies using ethnographic design can therefore be claimed to be problematic when it comes to the new insights they bring to the table. Researchers following narrative and descriptive writings will nevertheless argue that the narrative itself is the answer. This is an argument close to what Geertz called the interpretive success (Geertz, 1973b).

One example of narrative analysis from ethnographic field work in own practice, is the works of Vivian Gussin Paley (Paley, 1979, 1986, 1990, 1997). On one level the reader will get the didactic story of how she works with a story table, writing down children's narratives and giving the children opportunities for playing them out in structured drama activities as well as in by children's self-organised activities. At another level her stories can be read as auto-ethnographic accounts, where she critically reveals for the reader her continued reflections and self-shaping as a preschool teacher. Paley's descriptions of and reflections on teachers' approaches to children's stories are widespread in many Euro-American teacher communities and have inspired researchers to investigate children's social and textual lives in classrooms (Dyson, 1997; Palludan, 2007; Sawyer, 1997; Ødegaard, 2007, 2011a).

In her first auto-ethnographic accounts (Paley, 1986a, 1986b, 1990), the methodological issues discussed are limited, even if the self-reflection, self-presentation and work in progress is present. In her book *Kwanzaa and me—a teacher's story* (Paley, 1995), she describes a process of self-reflection over practice in her own classroom. In this account she foregrounds the critique raised towards her earlier narratives and her interpretation of what was going on and how she wrote about the children and her play-based curriculum and practice. Paley writes an auto-ethnographic account opening the narrative with the story about the teacher assistant confronting Paley with how she had narrated stories about her and incidents that she also had experienced. So Paley responds to critique of earlier ethnographic research work in this publication. By looking back with the insights from recent methodological discussions, she takes up issues of reliability such as the impact of context, the account's agenda, the author's/researcher's rationale for choices made, contact with people to establish a motive for participating, trustworthiness and so on.

Even if such a posttransparency gives insights and inspiration for new views, reliability issues concerning empirical narrative analytic work are usually not elaborated in pedagogical ethnographies within the early childhood field. Both phenomenological as well as poststructural academic writings have elaborated self-reflexive analysis of the relationships between the researcher and the participants, where the researcher meets in the field (Atkinson, 2001; Atkinson & Delamont, 2008; Cannella, 1997; Charmaz & Mitchell, 1997; Delamont, 2002; Hatch, 2007). Considering the way we work analytically and the way we write up cases can illuminate relationships between text and context, analytic work, transcription based on video analysis and field notes, the process of transcription and coding and the researcher's understanding of this process.

ANALYSIS OF CHILDREN'S NARRATIVE PLAY

Studies of children's narrative play will often be inspired by methods from anthropology, where thick description is used to capture children's imaginary narrative play in writing. Video observation and video transcripts are widely used.

When researching close to and along with children, it soon becomes obvious that children tell stories where the narrative can be seen as inspired by real events. Narrative play can be studied as children's culture, fiction, representations and potential reality. The foci point is merely children's artistic activities, their imaginative play, gaming and virtual reality.

Brian Sutton Smith states that the word *imaginary* means to be not real, fanciful and visionary (Sutton-Smith, 1997, p. 127). He traces the origin of such research to romanticism, art, literature and semiotics. Approaching play and possible worlds with narrative analysis, could be said to be following the root of pragmatism and transformed and intertwined with other roots. Whether something is true or false, can represent something else or should mean anything particular for someone, can be more or less of interest and addressed accordingly. Fiction, gaming and play can be studied in relation to other texts and so-called reality contexts. Fiction, gaming and play can, however, create narratives where whether it is true or false is of no interest. Play is then considered as a possible world or like an explorative improvisation, preparation or a dream. Bruner makes the distinction between two modes of thought, a paradigmatic and a narrative way of reasoning (Bruner, 1986). The paradigmatic mode is characterised by logic, as in the process of building arguments, while the narrative mode concerns people's intentional actions and experiences. Different possibilities for understanding, meaning-making, remembering and construction of knowledge derive from these modes. Research occupied with studying children's narrative play, we believe, will see some sort of transformation in the analysis.

The telling from the perspective of the child or for giving children voice or representation could moreover be studied in non-verbal approaches like the modality of the moving body and the rhythm in dance, representing as in picturing, visual as in photography and film and virtual as in creating stories in data programs and gaming.

In Annica Löfdahl's study about play in kindergarten (Löfdahl, 2002) imaginative play episodes and both field notes, audio and video recordings were used. She included children in her process of making, analysing and understanding play events by asking children to comment upon the play during breaks in play. She also stopped the video camera, rewound and showed the children still photos from the imaginative play that had just happened. She chose to show still photos rather than video with sound because she had experienced that children would extend their telling more if they did not listen to themselves talking and playing. She approached the analytic process as a co-construction between the researcher and the group of children, a meta text was taped and added to the analysis of the narrative play. This added contextual information to the analysis (Löfdahl, 2002, p. 56–63).

Following a dramaturgic analytic model (Heggstad, Knudsen, & Trageton, 1994) and using concepts deriving from theatre and drama, the study found small children's play as an arena for social and cultural meaning-making.

Løfdahl Found Two Mayor Themes in the Play:

1. *Survival.* How the children gestalted excitement and fairy tale, to be left alone and leave and to solve problems.
2. *Hegemonies.* How the children gestalted to be small and big, to be right and wrong and to be forceful or powerless.

Inspired by an analytic model traced to theatre and drama as referred to above (Heggstad, Knudsen, & Trageton, 1994), we suggest some added questions for an analytic process of the narrative data in studies of children's play:

1. In order to shed light on the narrative play drama as content:
   What is the fable about and what do the figures do?
   Where is the narrative play situated?
   When is it taken place?
2. In order to shed light on the narrative play drama as process and result:
   How the children shape their imaginative play worlds?
   How is the excitement constructed?
   Are there any rituals? Rhythms? Symbols? Costumes? Play artefacts? Sounds? Lightening? Under texts?
3. In order to shed light on narrative play drama as form, type or style:
   How do children tell their stories?
   What kinds of stories are told?
   Is it absurd? Socio-realistic? Expressionistic?

SOCIOLINGUISTIC NARRATIVE ANALYSIS

Within the field of sociolinguistics we find origins back to the work of Propp's (1968) study of Russian folktales and some would also say to Labov (Labov, 1972). Within this tradition researchers have been working with questions like:

- What is a narrative?
- How can we tell that this data that we have collected or constructed is a narrative?
- What form do stories have?
- What functions do they have?
- And how are they used by participants in the research project?

Stories are said to hold a form with beginnings, middles and endings (Thornborrow & Coates, 2005). Children's narratives are studied with focus on identifying the basic structural elements used by children in narration. Attempts are here made to link children's narrative abilities to the development of cognitive skills and are often related to aspects of sense-making and learning. The premise here is that children's narratives become 'more complete' as they get older. Children learning to narrate can be characterised as their stories move from brief, non-causally linked descriptions to more sophisticated, causally-linked stories as they grow older. According to studies in this tradition, where age has been considered important, young children will most frequently tell personal stories, while older children will add fantasy stories to their evolving narrative repertoire (Glenn-Applegate, Breit-Smith, Justice, & Piasta, 2010). Another example of this research tradition is McCabe and Peterson's study, based on Labov and Waletzky's (1967) structural analysis, with the main interest in mapping the function of clauses and how children link together a series of clauses that build up to a high point (McCabe & Peterson, 1991b).

Research concerned with narrative development has often been designed and studied in parent-child dyads (often mother-child). These studies have shown how maternal conversational discourse shapes children's use of genres and that dedicated mothers that engage their children in lengthy (narrative) conversations where they ask open-ended questions, provide narrative structure and supply rich information guides for their children to develop decontextualized language, a skill sociolinguistic researchers claim is necessary for successful schooling (Boyce, Innocenti, Roggman, Norman, & Ortiz, 2010; Reesea, Leyvab, Sparksc, & Grolnick, 2010; Schicka & Melzia, 2010).

This tradition is often connected to didactics aiming at school readiness in talking, reading and writing in education, where researchers' work also includes reflections on didactic approaches for eliciting children's stories in teacher-led activities and discussions and making suggestions on how to organise rich language, narrative and literacy classrooms (Dickinson, 2001; Dyson, 1997; Gjems, 2006; Ochs & Capps, 2001; Pramling & Ødegaard, 2011). There is consensus among researchers that teachers should be close to children for an extended period of time in a language activity or during everyday activities and routine situations (Aukrust, 2006; McCabe & Peterson, 1991a, 1991b), as this conditions situations for telling, listening, writing and imaging and picturing stories.

NARRATIVE DIALOGIC ANALYSIS

This approach takes especially into consideration how play, activity and talk is dialogically produced and performed as narrative. Here the *who* is of special interest in the analysis. Who is the utterance addressed to? And what are the relations between the utterances as they go about a person or a group? The context from where the utterance is performed is crucial. Utterances are fundamentally relational. They are performed from a certain position or perspective that is different from the one who listens. An utterance will be seen as a historical event, every utterance will have traces of many authors as every utterance is structured with ideology from previous usage. Form and meaning emerge between people in social practices and narratives can be seen as dialogical events. In educational institutions a story will be considered as co-produced in a complex choreography—in spaces between teller and listener, speaker and setting, text and reader (Riessman, 2008). The meaning of a narrative will therefore be considered diverse.

Asking children their opinion or listening to their initiatives and bodily movements are approaches already recognized as narrative research approaches in theme analysis, data from interviews and ethnographic accounts. The complex natures of early childhood settings challenge the researcher when it comes to researching the youngest children's cultural formation, their perspectives, meaning-making, identity in everyday (play and learning) activities. When it comes to the youngest children, more methodological exploration is needed. In order to research how children participate and make meaning and how they participate in shaping local practices in the early childhood institutions from a very young age, co-narrative approaches were methodologically explored in the thesis *Narrative meaning-making in preschool* (Ødegaard, 2007). In a poststudy further investigations where organized around how to study children as cultural subjects in a web of structural and relational conditions. Observations from kindergarten activities in a co-operating fieldwork design included a combination of collaborative narrative and visual approaches and so on. The project follows officially recommended ethical considerations. Parents and staff have given their informed consent. Collaborative co-narrative combined with picture activities as photos and drawings. are experienced as an appropriate tool in researching very young children in institutional practice. Experiencing the practice of collaborative design with young children, studying co-narration and co-picture-making give dynamic and new insights and knowledge. The collaborative intergenerational view goes beyond listening to children's own perspectives. Meaning-making is rather seen dialogically constructed in socio-historical-cultural endeavours.

Narratives are seen as multi-voiced and as a consequence must be analysed as poly vocal. In a recent comparative study of preschool teachers' practice in Norway and China, how the idea(l)s of individualization are constituted in preschool teachers' practice was explored (Birkeland, 2012). Both researcher and kindergarten teachers used photos/videos as prompts in focus group interviews. This approach to narrative analysis contributes to collaboration in meaning-making between researcher and the interviewed. Findings showed that multi-vocal interpretations of the teachers' practices, where photo elicitation can contribute to convey the hyper complexity of kindergarten teachers' educational preferences. Further on, a poly vocal approach gave opportunities for rich descriptions and a nuanced understanding of how cultural values influence the interpretations of the everyday curriculum in the educational institution.

With Bakhtin as inspiration a number of educational researchers have told stories from teachers' classrooms. Despite the fact that Bakhtin himself practiced as a teacher and teacher educator, there is not any own Bakhtin's philosophy of teaching. There are still a number of scientists worldwide that allows Bakhtin's philosophy inform studies in pedagogical field (see for example Matusov, 2011; White, 2009; White & Peters, 2011). Bakhtin's rich conceptual framework has been followed both to show how teaching takes place within complex relationships and how these are related to issues of social, historical, ideological and political character. Bakhtin's rich conceptual framework has inspired various analyses used here, for example, the term *author* (Matusov, 2011), *Carnival* (Lensmire, 2011) and *kronotop* (Ødegaard, 2011b).

CONCLUSION

In this chapter we have unfolded some traditions in narrative methodology relevant for studying contemporary early childhood education and children's events situated there. The field is wide and the borders between the narrative traditions are blurred. While it is considered fairly easy to encourage people (that is, adults) to tell their stories (Baden & Major, 2013, p. 239), it may not be the same situation when working with children. Narratives about children must encourage the researcher to design studies where appropriate caution for the gathering and production of narrative data and ethics are taken. We have chosen some narrative approaches commonly used in the field of early childhood educational studies. From some selected examples we have followed origins and paradigms and briefly given some foundations for narrative analysis and analysis of narratives. The examples are following a postclassical trace where a narrative analysis is presented as a process where stories are seen as a co-construction and put together by the researcher.

NOTE

[1]   Could mean originality.

REFERENCES

Atkinson, P. (2001). *Handbook of ethnography*. London: Sage.

Aukrust, V. G. (2006). *Tidlig språkstimulering og livslang læring: en kunnskapsoversikt*. Oslo: Departementet.

Savin-Baden, M., & Major, C. H. (2013). *Qualitative research: The essential guide to theory and practice*. New York, NY: Routledge.

Bakhtin, M. M. (1986). The problem of speech genres (V. W. McGee, Trans.). In C. H. Emerson & M. Holquist (Ed.), *Speech genres and other late essays* (2002 ed.). Austin, TX: University of Texas Press.

Birkeland, L. (1998). *Pedagogiske erobringer: om praksisfortellinger og vurdering i barnehagen.* Oslo: Pedagogisk forum.

Birkeland, L. (2007). *Den gjennomsiktige barnehagen—pedagogisk dokumentasjon.* Bergen: Fagbokforlaget.

Bourdieu, P., & Wacquant, L. J. D. (1992). *An invitation to reflexive sociology.* Cambridge: Polity Press.

Boyce, L., Innocenti, M., Roggman, L., Norman, V. K. J., & Ortiz, E. (2010). Telling stories and making books: Evidence for an intervention to help parents in migrant head start families support their children's language and literacy. *Early Education & Development, 21*(3), 343–371.

Bruner, J., & Lucariello, J. (1989). Monologue as narrative recreation of the world. In K. Nelson (Ed.), *Narratives from the crib* (pp. 73–98). Cambridge, MA: Harvard University Press.

Bruner, J. S., Feldman, C. F., Hermansen, M., & Molin, J. (2006). *Narrative, learning and culture.* Copenhagen: New Social Science Monographs.

Chase, S. E. (2011). Narrative inquiry: Still a field in the making. In N. K. Denzin & Y. S. Lincoln (Eds.), *The sage handbook of qualitative research.* Thousand Oaks: Sage.

Clandinin, D. J., & Connelly, F. M. (2000). *Narrative inquiry: Experience and story in qualitative research.* San Francisco, CA: Jossey-Bass.

Clandinin, D. J., & Rosiek, J. (2007). Mapping a landscape of narrative inquiry. In D. J. Clandinin (Ed.), *Handbook of narrative inquiry: Mapping a methodology.* Thousand Oaks, CA: Sage Publication.

Craig, C. J. (2007). Story constellations: A narrative approach to contextualizing teachers' knowledge of school reform. *Teacher and teacher education, 23,* 173–188.

Czarniawska, B. (2004). The uses of narrative in social science research. In M. B. Hardy & A. Bryman (Ed.), *Handbook of data analysis.* Thousand Oaks, CA: Sage Publications.

Dickinson, D. K. T., & Patton, O. (Ed.). (2001). *Beginning literacy with language* (2002 ed.). Baltimore, MD: Paul H. Brooks Publishing Co.

Dore, J. (1989). Monologue as reenvoicement of dialogue. In K. Nelson (Ed.), *Narratives from the crib* . Cambridge, MA: Harvard University Press.

Dyson, A. H. (1997). *Writing superheroes: Contemporary childhood, popular culture, and classroom literacy.* New York, NY: Teachers College Press.

Feldman, C. F. (1989). Monologue as problem solving narrative. In K. Nelson (Ed.), *Narratives from the crib* (pp. 98–102). Cambridge, MA: Harvard University Press.

Garvis, S., & Dwyer, R. (2013). *Whisperings from the corridors: Stories of teachers in higher education.* Rotterdam: Sense Publisher.

Gerhardt, J. (1989). Monologue as speech genre. In K. Nelson (Ed.), *Narratives from the crib* (pp. 171–230). Cambridge, MA: Harvard University Press.

Gjems, L. (2006). *Hva lærer barn når de forteller?: en studie av barns læringsprosesser gjennom narrativ praksis.* Oslo: Pedagogisk forskningsinstitutt, Det utdanningsvitenskapelige fakultet, Universitetet i Oslo.

Glenn-Applegate, K., Breit-Smith, A., Justice, L. M., & Piasta, S. B. (2010). Artfulness in young children's spoken narratives. *Early Childhood Development, 21*(3), 468–493.

Grenfell, M. (Ed.). (2008). *Pierre Bourdieu.* Stocksfield: Acumen.

Heggstad, K. M., Knudsen, I. M., & Trageton, A. (1994). *Fokus på lek estetikk, progresjon, kultur.* Stord: Høgskolen Stord/Haugesund.

Herman, L., & Vervaeck, B. (2001). *Handbook of narrative analysis.* Antwerpen: Vantil & Vubpress.

Hyvarinen, M., Hyden, L.-C., & Saarenheimo, M. (2010). *Beyond narrative coherence.* Amsterdam: John Benjamins Publishing Co.

Labov, W. (1972). *Sociolinguistic patterns.* Philadelphia, PA: University of Pennsylvania Press.

Labov, W., & Waletzky, J. (2006). Narrative analysis: Oral versions of personal experience. In P. Cobley (Ed.), *Communication theories: Critical concepts in media and cultural studies* (Vol. 3, pp. 28–63). London: Routledge.

Lensmire, T. J. (2011). Too serious—learning, schools, and Bakhtin's Carnival. In E. J. P. White & A. Michael (Ed.), *Bakhtinian pedagogy: Opportunities and Challenges for research, policy and practice in education across the globe.* New York, NY: Peter Lang.

Matusov, E. (2011). Authorial teaching and learning. In E. J. White & M. Peters (Eds.), *Bakhtinian pedagogy.* New York, NY: Peter Laing Publication.

McCabe, A., & Peterson, C. (1991a). Getting the story: A longitudinal study of parental styles in eliciting narratives and developing narrative skill. In A. McCabe & C. Peterson (Eds.), *Developing narrative structure*. Hillsdale, NJ: Lawrence Erlbaum Associates, Publisher.

McCabe, A., & Peterson, C. (Eds.). (1991b). *Developing narrative structure*. Hillsdale, NJ: Lawrence Erlbaum Associates Publisher.

Nelson, K. (1989a). Monologue as the linguistic construction of self in time. In K. Nelson (Ed.), *Narratives from the crib* (pp. 289–309). Cambridge, MA: Harvard University Press.

Nelson, K. (2006). *Narratives from the crib: With a new foreword by Emily Oster, the child in the crib*. Cambridge, MA: Harvard University Press.

Nelson, K. (Ed.). (1989b). *Narratives from the crib*. Cambridge, MA: Harvard University Press.

Ochs, E., & Capps, L. (2001). *Living narrative: Creating lives in everyday storytelling*. Cambridge, MA: Harvard University Press.

Paley, V. G. (1979). *White teacher*. Cambridge, MA: Harvard University Press.

Paley, V. G. (1986). *Boys and girls: Superheroes in the doll corner*. Chicago, IL: University of Chicago press.

Paley, V. G. (1990). *The boy who would be a helicopter*. Cambridge, MA: Harvard University Press.

Paley, V. G. (1997). *The girl with the brown crayon*. Cambridge, MA: Harvard University Press.

Palludan, C. (2007). Two tones: The core of inequality in kindergarten. *International Journal of Early Childhood, 39*(1), 75–93.

Pinnegar, S., & Daynes, J. G. (2007). Locating narrative inquiry historically. In D. J. Clandinin (Ed.), *Handbook of narrative inquiry:Mapping a methodology*. Thousand Oaks, CA: Sage Publication.

Polkinghorne, D. E. (1988). *Narrative knowing and the human sciences*. Albany, NY: State University of New York Press.

Polkinghorne, D. E. (1995). Narrative configuration in qualitative analysis. In J. A. Hatch (Ed.), *Life history and narrative*. London: Routledge Falmer.

Pramling, N., & Ødegaard, E. E. (2011). Learning to narrate: Appropriating a cultural mould for sense-making and communication. In N. Pramling & I. P. Samuelsson (Ed.), *Educational encounters: Nordic studies in early childhood didactics*. New York, NY: Springer

Pramling, N., & Ødegaard, E. E. (2014). Berättande och minnande. In B. Bruce & B. Riddarsporre (Eds.), *Berättande i förskolan*. Stockholm: Natur och Kultur.

Reesea, E., Leyvab, D., Sparksc, A., & Grolnick, W. (2010). Maternal elaborative reminiscing increases low-income children's narrative skills relative to dialogic reading. *Early Education and Development, 21*(3), 318–342.

Riessman, C. K. (2008). *Narrative methods for the human sciences*. Los Angeles, CA: Sage Publications.

Sawyer, K. R. (1997). *Pretend play as improvisation: Conversation in the preschool classroom*. Mahwah, NJ: Lawrence Erlbaum Associates, Publishers.

Schicka, A., & Melzia, G. (2010). The development of children's oral narratives across contexts. *Early Education and Development, 21*(3), 293–317.

Stenensen, J. (2007). Biografiske interviews i kritisk realsitsisk perspektiv. In K. A. Petersen, S. Glasdam, & V. Lorentzen (Eds.), *Livshistorie-forskning og kvalitative interview*. Viborg: Forlaget PUC.

Stern, D. (1989). Crib Monologue from a psychoanalytic perspective. In K. Nelson (Ed.), *Narratives from the crib* (pp. 309–320). Cambridge, MA: Harvard University Press.

Sutton-Smith, B. (1997). *The ambiguity of play*. Cambridge, MA: Harvard University Press.

Thornborrow, J., & Coates, J. (2005). *The sociolinguistics of narrative*. Amsterdam: John Benjamins Pub. Co.

Watson, R. (1989). Monologue, dialogue and regulation. In K. Nelson (Ed.), *Narratives from the crib* (pp. 263–284). Cambridge, MA: Harvard University Press.

Webster, L., & Mertova, P. (2007a). *Using narrative inquiry as a research method*. New York, NY: Routledge.

Webster, L., & Mertova, P. (2007b). *Using narrative inquiry as a research method: An introduction to using critical event narrative analysis in research on learning and teaching*. London: Routledge.

Wells, C. G. (1987). *The meaning makers: Children learning language and using language to learn*. London: Hodder and Stoughton.

White, E. J. (2009). *Assessment in New Zealand early childhood education: A Bakhtinian analysis of toddler metaphoricity* (Unpublished doctoral dissertation). Monash University, Victoria.

White, E. J., & Peters, M. (2011). *Bakhtinian pedagogy: Opportunities and challenges for research, policy and practice in education across the globe.* New York, NY: Peter Lang.

Wilson, D. E., & Ritchie, J. S. (2000). *Teacher narrative as critical inquiry: Rewriting the script.* New York, NY: Teachers College Press.

Ødegaard, E. E. (2007). *Meningsskaping i barnehagen: innhold og bruk av barns og voksnes samtalefortellinger.* Göteborg: Göteborgs universitet.

Ødegaard, E. E. (2011a). Narrative practice as a site for studying conditions for children's cultural formation. In Krogh-Hansen (Ed.), *Working with stories. Narrative as a meeting place for theory, analysis and practice: Proceedings from the 2nd ENN Conference.* Kolding: European Narratology Network.

Ødegaard, E. E. (2011b). On the track of cultural formative practice: A chronotopic reading of young children's co-narrative meaning making. In E. J. White & M. Peters (Ed.), *Bakhtinian pedagogy: Opportunities and challenges for research, policy and practice in education across the globe.* New York, NY: Peter Lang.

Ødegaard, E. E., & Birkeland, L. (2002). *Tusen erfaringer søker fortellinger -gleder og utfordringer med fortellinger i barnehagens pedagogiske arbeid* (2002 ed., Vol. 2). Bergen: Høgskolen i Bergen.

Ødegaard, E. E., & Økland, M. S. (Eds.). (2015, March). *Fortellinger fra praksis—profesjonalitet, identitet og barnehagelærerutdanning.* Bergen: Fagbokforlaget.

Elin Eriksen Ødegaard
Centre of Educational Research
Bergen University College

FUTURE CHALLENGES FOR NARRATIVE RESEARCH

INTRODUCTION

When considering narrative there are a number of different meanings and assertions that are commonly associated including the terms narrative research, narrative inquiry, and narrative analysis (Kuntay & Ervin-Tripp, 1997). As Bamberg (2012) shares:

> One of the most central ways this complexity plays out is in what can be taken as the most basic intersection, namely between research *on* narratives, where narratives are the object of study, and research *with* narratives, where narratives are the tools to explore something else—typically aspects of human memory or experience. (p. 112)

There is a story and varied history of narrative methods, as outlined in Chapter 1. Although originally founded in the Aristotle examination of Greek tragedy, Riessman (2008, p. 4) so eloquently reminds us that the tragic narrative:

> …is complete and whole of a certain amplitude (size)… [with] a classic structure with a beginning, middle, and an end (sequence rather than haphazard organization). There is a plot, the ordering of incidents, which constitutes the life blood of the narrative, and plot is enacted by characters, who tale a second place. It is the plot that awakens emotions, such as fear and dread, when things happen unexpectedly. Something goes awry: there is a breach in the expected state of things (*peripeteia*) that awakens response in the audience.

We are reminded though that as time has progressed, so too has our sense and perceived value of narrative—especially in the field of research. "Among serious scholars working in the social science with personal (first person) accounts for research purposes, there is a range of definitions of narratives, often linked to discipline" (Riessman, 2008, p. 5). But whatever the lens, the content and stories demand consequential linking of ideas or events. The narrative shaping thus "entails imposing a meaningful pattern on what would otherwise be random and disconnected" (Riessman, 2008, p. 5).

The diversity of how narrative is interpreted and applied presents complexities. For educational research and early childhood context we are reminded of the place of voice—researcher, practitioner, psychologist, parent, family, and indeed the young person themselves.

Narrative provides meaning and belonging in human lives because every human experience is a lived story, and a storied experience (Curtis & Carter, 2000; Wong, 2003). Connelly and Clandinin (1988) define narrative inquiry as "the study of how humans make meaning of experience by endlessly telling and retelling stories about themselves that both refigure the past and create purpose in the future" (p. 21). Most importantly working as a narrative inquirer is seen as "providing opportunities and spaces for research participants as well as researchers" (Bathmaker & Harnett, 2010, p. 3) which is an action as Riessman (2008) suggests that encourages and supports people to tell their stories and thus allows participants to negotiate their identities and meaning making of their experiences. The untold and unsayable stories can be shared (Leitch, 2008) as to those that are evaded (Bach, 1998) and those with covers (Clandinin & Connelly, 1995). As an increasing number of people throughout the world, and from a broad range of disciplines, are turning to narrative as a research methodology (Trahar, 2011) it is important to acknowledge the strengths as well as areas that specifically need to be addressed especially when working with young people, especially in early childhood.

"Learning to think with stories highlights the relational, multiperspectival processes in which participants and narrative inquirers inquire into their lived experiences and tell stories" (Clandinin, Huber, Steeves & Li, 2011, p. 33). To assist narrative inquirers as they face these representational complexities Connelly & Clandinin (2006) describe considerations that may be helpful including:

> …that as a narrative inquirer writes, they need to continue to think narratively, crafting the research text with careful attention to the narrative inquiry commonplaces. The text needs to reflect the temporal unfolding of people, places and things within the inquiry, the personal and social aspects of the inquirer's and participants' lives, and the places in the inquiry. (p. 485)

Research of recent has advocated for the honouring of voice and narrative as a way to explore and represent lived experiences (Castelle, 1990; Clarke & Moss, 2001; Curts & Carter, 2000; Kellet & Ding, 2004; Lemon, 2008; MacNaughton, 2003b; Malaguzzi, 1998; Mauthner, 1997). There has been considerable "global interest in the potential for public investments in early childhood care and education to improve the development of young children" (Barnett & Nores, 2012, p. 1).

> This interest is based on evidence of the importance of environmental influences on early cognitive and social development, the human and economic costs of poor developmental trajectories for children in poverty, and the potential for early interventions to alter those developmental trajectories. (Barnett & Nores, 2012, p. 1)

The use of narratives may provide early childhood educators with an alternative resource for understanding and considering the experiences of young students (Prior, 2013). Specifically noting that the value of narrative to unpack detail and uncover insights is a useful approach to identify knowledge gaps (Åkerman (2012). A narrative approach provides a place for the valuing of children's stories to provide educators a valuable resource for understanding the meaning children make of initial cross-cultural experience. This book invites educators and researchers to consider narrative as a meaningful and purposeful way to interact with the voice of young people. As an increasing number of people throughout the world – and from a broad range of disciplines – are turning to narrative as a research methodology (Trahar, 2011) it is important to consider the what, how and why of the types of narratives that wish to be engaged with and how they represent young people, their lived experiences, voices and unsayable stories. This book invites one to consider narratives for, with, about, by, between, and without children. The importance of narrative research for early childhood education will be discussed. The chapter will explore different types of narrative methodology for the future as children's documented learning moves beyond the realms of observation.

This chapter is presented with interweaving sections that discuss issues around challenges for narrative researchers in early childhood education specifically focusing on needs for early childhood education research/educators. Honouring of the voice of young people is highlighted, as too beginning the discussion about needs, including care and compassion, for early childhood education in moving forward while working in narrative research. Questions are posed throughout the chapter about ethical considerations, selection of methods, analysis and participation for young people, educators and researchers. These are seen as beginning points to trigger considerations for future movement forward in working with narratives and young people.

VOICE—HOLISTIC CALLS FOR ACKNOWLEDGING YOUNG CHILDREN AND THEIR VOICE

Thinking with "stories highlights the relational, multiperspectival processes in which participants and narrative inquirers inquire into their lived and told stories" (Clandinin, Huber, Steeves & Li, 2011, p. 33). To assist narrative inquirers as they face these representational complexities, Connelly & Clandinin (2006) describe considerations that may be helpful for the narrative inquirer:

> …continue to think narratively, crafting the research text with careful attention to the narrative inquiry commonplaces. The text needs to reflect the temporal unfolding of people, places and things within the inquiry, the personal and social aspects of the inquirer's and participants' lives, and the places in the inquiry. (p. 485)

Globally there is a call to acknowledge young children in educational practice and research (for example Alanen et al., 2005; Curtis & Carter, 2000; Lemon, 2008; MacNaughton, 2003a; 2003b). However, accompanying these persistent calls there is also confusion about what this is and what this looks like. As Kirby, Lanyon Cronin & Sinclair (2003) reiterate "the growing acceptance of the principle of young people's involvement has led, in recent years, to a mushrooming of participation activity" (p. 3). There are also issues around much of the participation activity highlighting the value of student voice or honouring student voice methods is one-off, or isolated, rather than embedded within agencies (Kirby, et al., 2003).

Considerations for moving forward are strongly connected to visions of how to improve human society by helping children realise their full potential as intelligent, creative, whole persons. Children are thus viewed as active authors or communicators of their lived experiences who can represent their own development, strongly influenced by natural, dynamic, self-righting forces within themselves, opening the way toward growth and learning. Partnering with adults such as teachers and parents careful consideration of learning environments supports theses notions. As to pedagogical decisions that support and provide strong messages about the curriculum and about respect for children are called upon. In valuing children for their perspective, partnering with parents is highly valued (Arthur et al., 2012). Underlying these approaches are variant views of the nature of young children's needs, interests, and modes of learning that lead to contrasts in the ways that teachers interact with children in the classroom, frame and structure learning experiences for children, and follow the children through observation/documentation (Kirby, et al., 2003).

How can you value young people's voice within the learning environment?
How does valuing student voice look in the learning environment?

When we are looking at the working with young people, representing young people, and thus honouring young people, there are various frameworks internationally that maintain that children and childhood are important own their own right (Tayler, 2012). The Australian National Early Years Learning Framework, for example, builds on the United National Convention on the Rights of the Child. This framework builds of principles and practices for children and presents that children:

- Have a strong sense of identity,
- Are connected with and contribute to their world,
- Have a strong sense of wellbeing,
- Are confident and involved learners, and
- Are effective communicators.

These are focuses that are echoed throughout other policy documents and the work of, for example, Lancaster & Kirby (2010) who advocate that listening to children within wider professional setting is required, and most importantly that "meaningful participation is a process, not simply the application of isolated, one-off participation activities or events" (Kirby, et al., 2003, p. 3).

Rodd (1994) argues that research does not provide magical answers for the early childhood sector, rather it can assist in advancing knowledge, challenging one's standpoint and help find new ways to view practice (Kreig, 2003; MacNaughton, 2003b; Robbins, 2003). In recent years Australian early childhood education researchers, who embrace the notion of multiple perspectives, have asked 'Where does the child fit within the research agenda? (Kilderry et al., 2004; Marshall, 2006; MacNaughton et al., 2006). Moreover, acknowledgment has also been made of practitioners expressing their want for local evidence-based research to support their pedagogical practices (Fleer, 2000). Recent Australian literature in the early childhood field indicates collaborative projects are generating much needed discussion about pedagogical practices (Fleer, 2000; Yellend, 2001; Raban, 2000; MacNaughton et al., 2006).

Fielding (2002), for example, suggests a refocusing on the centrality of relationships in education, collaborative learning spaces and opportunities for collective dialogue. He contends that the challenge is to build relationships and environments that support and sustain both student and teacher voice. Fielding recognizes a move towards constructing practices that create new spaces for teachers and students to make meaning both individually and collectively, stating that:

> …the voices of students, teachers and others are acknowledged as legitimately different and of equal value, the necessary partners in dialogue about how we learn, how we live and the kind of place we wish our community to become. (p. 13)

Using student voice is not only an instructional method for enhancing learning and motivation but also a way to enhance practice-orientated analytical approaches (Hadfield & Haw, 2001; Clarke, 2002). As Britzman (1990) notes, there is a need to acknowledge authenticity with regard to child voice, and it is important to recognise that voice is meaning which resides in the individual and enables the individual to participate in a community.

Dennis Harper (2003) reiterates that listening to children in meaningful partnerships with adults is foundational for addressing issues central to the empowerment of young people and for changing many system inequities and failures. This argument is endorsed by Hadfield and Haw (2001) who write:

> 'Voice' is now used in a wide variety of projects and policies from advocacy to consumer rights and citizenship education. The 'voice' of young people is being increasingly sought as part of the general move towards social inclusion. (p. 485)

Cook-Sather (2002) concurs and claims that children not only have the knowledge and position to shape what counts in education but they can help change power relationships and create new forums about learning through their active engagement in research processes.

In developing young peoples balanced development and their potentials, children's interests, experiences, abilities, needs and individual differences must be considered (Essa, 1999). A holistic view of children, including their social, emotional, cognitive and physical needs, requires careful consideration in future considerations about narrative representation. In thinking about narrative to share the voice and actions of young people the context that is representative of established research problems in the field, needs to also reflect newer areas of inquiry and "observations of children—their actions, language" (Roskos & Christie, 2001, p. 69). Education practices in centres and learning environments can focus on the child through a network of social stories, shaping personality through the use of specific pedagogies and strategies in an effort to build a cohesive community. In this way, early childhood institutions provide experiences beyond the family, enabling children to interact with others beyond their immediate community, providing a counterpoint to parental authority that consider the values and authority that are enacted within the relative positions of parents/families and institutions. A narrative identity is neither stable nor seamless. Rather, it is a complex array of stories about one's self in relation to others, entwined in history, community and memories. Just as it is possible to compose several plots about the same incidents "so it is always possible to weave different, even opposed, plots about our identities" (Ricœur, 1988, p. 248). Thus, Ricœur understands identity as being subject to experiences and instabilities and without a fixed identity.

In this way, Ricœur disproves the idea that the self is given to us, arguing that human actions are formed within social practices. This is not to say that a self is constituted by external obligation. Nor is narrative identity a deterministic view of self. Rather, the opposite is true: a narrative self is always a self-capable of creating something a new (Farquhar, 2012). There are a variety of ways to consider, value and enact narrative within early childhood education on way to honour the complexity of the "infant's looking and listening-in is illustrated and analysed through a visual narrative" (Sumsion & Goodfellow, 2012, p. 313). The use of visual narratives can highlight, for example, the complexity of one's meaning making and reinforces the importance of pedagogical practices that recognise and build on young people's "sophisticated capacities and structural conditions (for example, group size and adult-child ratios) in early childhood settings that support these practices" (Sumsion & Goodfellow, 2012, p. 325). Lemon's (2008) research, as explored in Chapter 7 also looks at how young children's voice generated through visual narratives is a powerful method that provides an alternative strategy for reflective learning by encouraging independence and accountability and by engaging children in authentic learning experiences.

VOICE—LISTENING, CONSULTATION AND PARTICIPATION

Working and researching in early childhood settings to inform our practice involves careful consideration of methodologies that explore new approaches towards childhood (Darbyshire et al., 2005; Mayall, 2000; O'Kane, 2000). As explored in Chapter 1, new directions for working with children need to recognise that children are capable meaning makers (Clark, McQuail & Moss, 2003; Lemon, 1998; Malaguzzi, 1998).

According to Greene (1995) listening, consultation and participation as part of a community "can happen even in the local spaces of the classroom, particularly when students are encouraged to find their voices and their images" (p. 39). Clark, McQuail & Moss (2003) in their work with children and practitioners in England

and Denmark in 50 sites recommended that "early years practitioners [need] to bring their knowledge about the ways young children think and communicate into debates around consulting children and children's participation" (p. 5). They reiterated that in honouring young people's voice, there is a need to listen "to young children needs to be part of a culture of listening which respects the views of adults and children" (p. 5). This raises important questions for moving forward in research *for*, *of*, *with*, and *about* young people and highlights the importance of debating the principles of listening.

What does it really mean when we are listening to young people?

What does listening to young people look like?

How can we enact listening to young people within our teaching and research agendas?

The research of Clark, McQuail & Moss (2003) identified two different purposes, with illustrating case study examples, for listening to and involving young children in education and childcare settings (pp. 6–8):

1. Everyday listening by those who regularly work with young children, giving opportunities for decision-making in routines and activities. This may include:

   • Prioritising time to listen to children talking, in groups and individually,
   • Using children's records of progress or 'profile books' as a daily listening tool,
   • 'Tuning in' routines to young children's rhythms, interests and developing skills,
   • Giving young children increasing control over their personal care,
   • Explaining, discussing and negotiating rules,
   • Seeking young children's opinions and solutions to problems which arise,
   • Developing ways of listening to and involving young children which open up more channels of communication with parents,
   • Designing personal 'passports' to listen to and empower young children with special needs, and
   • Taking part in a training program by a specialist organisation on listening to young children.

2. One-off consultation about a particular issue, event or opportunity. This may include:

   • Involving a Community Arts team to engage both parents and young children in consultations about a new building,
   • Involving older children to inform decisions about provision for children under four,
   • Employing an action researcher to involve young children in the planning and reviewing of services for parents and children.

Kirby et al. (2003) in their report of 29 sites in the UK identified that much activity that is centred on honouring the child is one-off, or isolated, rather than embedded within agencies. There are clear sustainability issues in work that is carried out about young people, with young people and for young people. Kirby, et al. (2003) superficially identifies important areas to consider as we move forward:

- Organisation to undertake meaningful and sustainable participation for change,
- Awareness around participation being a multi-layered concept, complex, and inclusive of all young people including valuing their contribution to decision-making,
- Meaningful participation is a process, not simply the application of isolated, one-off participation activities or events,
- Strategies designed to address both personal and public decision-making are needed to fulfil the rights of children and young people,
- Listening needs to influence change. Taking account of what children say is what makes their involvement meaningful,
- Acting on children and young people's views brings positive outcomes: in service developments, increasing young people's sense of citizenship and social inclusion, and enhancing their personal development, and
- There are different cultures of participation and organisations need to be clear about their reasons for undertaking participation and how they plan to develop this work into the future.

Narrative inquirers consider the particular methods they wish to use to study the phenomenon (Clandinin et al., 2007). In order to choose these methods narrative inquirers must first imagine what their inquiry will look like. They must consider addressing the phenomenon "along with possible participants, as existing in an ever shifting space" (Connelly & Clandinin, 2006, p. 481). Thinking about methods also means, "figuring out and describing the kind of field texts (narrative inquirers' term for data) [they] need to collect and compose" (Clandinin, et al., 2007, p. 27). These field texts may range from journal entries, field notes, photographs, and/or digital forms. However, inquirers must take the three commonplaces into consideration in order to ensure that the field texts are "attentive to all three" (p. 27).

RESPECT OF VOICE AND ETHICAL CONSIDERATIONS— CARE OF THE YOUNG PEOPLE

Respect of the closeness gained when listening to, sharing, and honouring the voice of young people must be acknowledged in directions moving forward associated to narrative inquiry. Noddings (2005) writes about the "ethics of care" and the importance of students experiencing relationships in educational settings and schools throughout their education. Central within this process is the concept of belonging associated to voice:

When students are taken seriously and attended to as knowledgeable participants in important conversations, they feel empowered and motivated to participate constructively in their education. (Cook-Sather, 2002, p. 3)

In regards to the impact of listening to young children, there is considerable evidence to the value at an individual, institutional and strategic level (Clark, McQuail & Moss (2003). Research indicates that young children can experience increased self-esteem and social competency, together with gaining an insight into decision-making processes, when they are respected while sharing their narratives (Lewis, 1993; Marshall, 1997; Target and Fonagy, 1996). At an individual level the impact of listening to young children can have an impact on parents and educators attitudes while also challenging perceptions of children's capabilities and insights (Lemon, 2008). It has also been noted that the impact at an institutional level has led in some instances to changes in policies and to designs of outdoor and indoor spaces (Thomson, 2009). There are however, few examples found of the impact of young children's views on change at a strategic level reinforcing future directions.

What is the impact on adults and educational institutions and policy when listening to young people's voices in respected and honored?

Why is voice not always valued?

How can voice be included in learning and teaching, curriculum design, and pedagogical decisions by educators?

Faulkner and Coates's (2011) work provides theoretical and practical insights into how to work with young children. They challenge traditional ways of viewing education by thinking about their creativity as a way to understand, hear, and investigate the perspective of young people. They argue that working with young people should be:

- Multimodal, social and collaborative,
- Challenge the view that young children's creativity and expression can only be judged in terms of their creative outputs of products, and
- Listening and engaging with voice is more important than focusing just on the process.

When we consider the future directions of how we can work with young children to highlight their development, voice and fresh new perspectives on meaning making. There are multiple ways to listen to voice (Kirby, 2010):

- Drawing, painting, making
- Drama and play
- Musical conversations
- Photos, film, audio, computers
- Toys, dolls and props
- Visual tools (e.g., happy/sad faces, walks)
- Observation
- Conversations and interviews
- Group discussions

Enabling practitioners to develop and offer young children real opportunities to communicate their experiences, views, concerns and aspirations (Lancaster & Kirby, 2010) is a challenge in the movement forward in early childhood education. Although in some countries from a macro perspective a variety of these ways of listening to and encouraging young people voice is a regular part of education and research-practitioner approaches, there are many centres, educational settings or learning environments that on the micro level may not nor know how to.

How can we open up the dialogue to learn from each other to embed children's voice into regular practice?

When listening to young people's voice to enable choice in how and what they share, Kirby et al. (2003) reminds us that it does not mean we provide unlimited choices and no structure. Rather that children need to learn to choose through meaningful experiences that are connected to real life choices. Underpinning this is support to understand choice and consequences while also supporting exploration into voice (Marchant & Kirby, 2004).

Children's participation in decision-making and problem solving while sharing their voice is a vital part of honouring young people. As much as it is about honouring the individual there are many different ways to ignite possibility to listen, hear, share perspective, and consider where to next. As Faulkner and Coates (2011) encourage children can communicate with others including adults and their meaning making can be constructed and mediated by all their previous historical moments of significant play. We can see that as with Kirby (2010) and Wright (2011) research suggests we can also learn from young people by seeing socio-dramatic play, dance, music making, as art making are valuable sources to hearing voices and thus generating narratives. These improvisational, reciprocal, and collaborative ways of meaning making challenge many traditional ways of communicating with young people and honouring their narratives. Although they are familiar as a part of the curriculum the implications for use for research are not fully explored. Through working these ways fundamental skills for learning, refection and metacognitive skills are engaged with, developed and enacted that enables young people to describe, explain and justify their thinking about different aspects of the world to others. Although they are familiar as a part of the curriculum the implications for use for research and methodology with young people in early childhood settings are not fully explored.

Greene (1995) supports the idea that community "can happen even in the local spaces of the classroom, particularly when students are encouraged to find their voices and their images" (p. 39). Thus, community:

...cannot be produced simply through rational formulation nor through edict
... it has to be achieved by persons offered the space in which to discover what they recognize together and appreciate in common. (Greene, 1995, p. 39)

Reading Greene's thoughts we can inquire and consider what may be needed to ensure students experience spaces in school where their voices, their images, their identities flourish. Smyth and Fasoli (2007) suggest that "earning [students'] respect [is] crucial to ensuring [students'] educational success" (p. 281). Furthermore, one way to earn students' respect is through conscious wakefulness to "relational power" (p. 283), which is a concept "generally used to refer to the way in which collaboration and trust is created across and among constituent groups in schools" (p. 283). In their work, Smyth and Fasoli highlight the need for teachers to consciously work to hear, and to understand, the stories students tell, the gifts students embody, and the struggles that shape the diverse lives of students.

ENTERING THE WORLD OF THE PARTICIPANTS AND SELECTING APPROPRIATE METHODS

Storied and gathering of stories must "not be treated lightly as they carry and inspire, significant obligations and responsibilities" (Huber et al., 2013, p. 214). As we read, listen, consider and ponder narratives we are invited to wonder:

> ...for example, about the possibilities for storying and restorying ourselves and one another into being; we wonder about new kinds of, or maybe forgotten or written over, obligations and ways of interacting and responding to with one another. (Huber et al., 2013, p. 216)

Teacher and child voice together can paint a bigger picture of perspective. For example Bedford & Casbergue (2012) employed a case study methodology in order to "unravel the teachers' decision-making, beliefs, and interactions throughout the day in an early years setting" while Odom & Strain (2002) reinforce approaches that child-focused practices. In moving forward actions need to careful consider entering the participants world including selecting appropriate methods.

Embedded closely to this action are choices that are authentic to the participants and also the setting. Working in activities that matter to the children and more in their terms and ecological context. Kirby (2010) invited the researcher and/or educator to consider:

- Asking the right questions,
- Avoid pressure, whilst meeting demands,
- Allow free talk, whilst getting answers,
- Precision,
- Accuracy, and
- Keeping focus on the child.

A Mosaic Approach (Clark and Moss 2001; Clark 2004; Clark 2005), which brings together visual and verbal research tools, can be engaged with as a way to highlight the strength of the pieces coming together for all "practitioners a particular insight into children's views or experiences…and a strength of this approach is in bringing these individual pieces together, through the process of dialogue, reflection and interpretation" (Clark & Moss, 2001, p. 11). This approach, often paired with participatory action research, has the children and young people participating as researchers and co-researchers to enable young children to share their views as a way to provide feedback to adults in various roles from various settings (Clark, 2010). This approach to listening doesn't need to be seen as an extra activity that takes up valuable curriculum time, because this is about learning. At one level, there is the potential for learning goals to be achieved through working with children in this way, for example, developing speaking and listening skills through using the cameras. At a deeper level, children are engaged in an active process of meaning making (Clark & Moss, 2001). Giving children and young people the chance to participate in making decisions can make a real difference not only to their educational experience but also to the impact children and young people can have in their communities. In this approach the children and young people are researchers as well as being researched about. They are being listened to and treated with respect by which we mean be able to have a say in all decisions, which affect them and have an understanding of their rights and responsibilities.

Sumsion & Goodfellow (2012) bring our attention to narratives that connect to young people's lifeworlds and thus honour reflexive thinking when interpreting their meaning. From a hermeneutic perspective there is unremarkable insight gained when an adult researcher looks and listens-in and connects to the reflexivity of the voice being shared. Nelson (2006) presents compelling evidence of narrative comprehension and construction, and implicitly reflexivity, in the monologues of a two-year-old child. "Conceivably, then, younger, pre-verbal infants could engage in narratively organised, unspoken monologues as a way of making sense of their experiences" (p. 316).

Are we asking the right questions to young people?

Can we ask the questions differently?

What methods can we access to honour children's meaning making and insights?

Are there repercussions?

Are the young people still figuring it out?

Is an adult putting value on something that the students do not?

These question invite a shifting of the audience for the narrator—to share narrative for self, for researcher, for child, for policy, and so on, can change what is shared and indeed how.

CONCLUSION

The use of narrative as a contemporary research technique allows young children to share their experiences, meaning making, and perspectives with others.

This chapter has provided an overview of issues around challenges for narrative researchers in early childhood education specifically focusing on needs for early childhood education research/educators and the honouring of the voice. Questions have been posed throughout the chapter and have been seen as beginning points to trigger considerations for future movement forward in working with narratives and young people. Throughout the book we invite you to consider how you can work with narratives for, with, about, by, between, and without children. It is hoped that the questions and ideas posed in this chapter assist with the approach to working with children in narrative ways. A wide range of activities and techniques can be used in interviews and focus groups with children that are enjoyable and interesting but still encourage the child to take control of the focus, agenda, and their voice. These approaches are central to allowing a sharing of understanding, knowledge and trust in the research approach.

REFERENCES

Åkerman, E. (2012). *Children's systems telling and the story of a meatball's social-ecological system: A narrative approach to systems thinking in early childhood education for sustainable development* (Masters dissertation). Stockholm University, Sweden. Retrieved from http://urn.kb.se/resolve?urn=urn:nbn:se:su:diva-79240

Alanen, L., Kiili, J., Kuukka, A., & Lehiten, A. R. (2005). Health, wellbeing and children's agency. In *GEMS of the health promotion research programme*. Tampere, Finland: Cancer Society of Finland and Academy of Finland.

Arthur, L., Beecher, B., Death, E., Dockett, S., & Farmer, S. (2012). *Programming and planning in early childhood settings*. Sydney: Cengage Learning.

Bach, H. (1998). *A visual narrative concerning curriculum, girls, photography etc*. Edmonton, Alberta, Canada: Qual Institute Press.

Bamberg, M. (2012). Narrative analysis. In H. Cooper (Ed.), *APA handbook of research methods in psychology* (pp. 111–130). Washington, DC: American Psychological Association Press.

Barnett, W. S., & Nores, M. (2012). *Investing in early childhood education: A global perspective*. New Brunswick, NJ: National Institute for Early Education Research, Rutgers The State University of New Jersey.

Bedford, A., & Casbergue, R. (2012). Research round-up. *Journal of Research in Childhood Education, 26*(1), 335–340.

Britzman, D. (1990). *Practice makes practice*. New York, NY: SUNY Press.

Castelle, K. (1990). *In the child's best interest: A primer on the U.N. Convention on the rights of the child*. East Greenwich, RI: Plan International.

Clandinin, D. J., & Connelly, F. M. (1995). *Teachers' professional knowledge landscapes*. New York, NY: Teachers College Press.

Clandinin, D.J., Huber, J., Steeves, P., & Li, Y. (2011). Becoming a narrative inquirer: Learning to attend within the three-dimensional narrative inquiry space. In S. Trahar (Ed.). *Learning and teaching narrative inquiry: Travelling in the borderlands* (pp. 33–52). Amsterdam, The Netherlands: John Benjamins Publishing Company.

Clarke, D. (2002, March). *Learner's perspective study: Exploiting the potential for complementary analyses*. Paper presented at the conference of American Educational Research Association, New Orleans.

Clark, A., McQuail, S., & Moss, P. (2003). *Exploring the field of listening to and consulting with young children*. London: Thomas Coram Research Unit.

Clark, A., & Moss, P. (2001). *Listening to young children: The Mosaic approach*. London: National Children's Bureau.

Connelly, F. M., & Clandinin, D. J. (1988). *Teachers as curriculum planners: Narratives of experience.* New York, NY: Teachers College, Columbia University.

Cook-Sather, A. (2002). Authorizing students' perspective: Toward trust, dialogue, and change in education. *Educational Researcher, 31*(4), 3 –14.

Curtis, D., & Carter, M. (2000). *The art of awareness: How observations can transform your teaching.* St Paul, MN: Redleaf Press.

Darbyshire, P., MacDougall, C., & Schiller, W. (2005). Multiple methods in qualitative research with children: More insight or just more? *Qualitative Research, 5*(4), 417–436.

Essa, E. (1999). *Introduction to early childhood education* (3rd ed.). Albany, NY: Delmar Publisher.

Farquhar, S. (2012). Narrative identity and early childhood education. *Educational Philosophy and Theory, 44*(3), 289–301.

Faulkner, D., & Coates, E. (2011). *Exploring children's creative narratives.* London: Routledge.

Fielding, M. (2002). *Beyond the rhetoric of student voice: New departures or new constraints in the transformation of 21st century schooling?* Paper presented at American Educational Research Association, New Orleans.

Fleer, M. (2000). *An early childhood research agenda: Voices from the field.* Canberra: JS McMillan.

Foucault, M. (1984). On the genealogy of ethics: An overview of work in progress. In P. Rabinow (Ed.). *The Foucault reader* (pp. 340–372). New York, NY: Pantheon.

Greene, M. (1993). Diversity and inclusion: Toward a curriculum for human beings. *Teachers College Record, 95*(2), 211–221.

Greene, M. (1995). *Releasing the imagination.* San Francisco, CA: Jossey-Bass Inc.

Hadfield, M., & Haw, K. (2001). 'Voice', young people and action research. *Educational Action Research, 9*(3), 485–499.

Harper, D. (2003). Students as change agents: The generation Y model. In M. S. Khine & D. Fisher (Eds.), *Technology-Rich learning environments: A future perspective* (pp. 307–330). New Jersey, NJ: World Scientific.

Kellett, M., & Ding, S. (2004). Middle childhood. In S. Fraser, V. Lewis, S. Ding, M. Kellet, & C. Robinsons (Eds.), *Doing research with children and young people* (pp. 161–174). London: The Open University.

Kilderry, A., Nolan, A., & Noble, K. (2004). Multiple ways of knowing and seeing on the renewed vigor in early childhood research. *Australian Journal of Early Childhood, 29*(2), 24–28.

Kirby, P. (2010, November 17). *Listening to children and the family justice review.* Coram Seminar. Retrieved June 26, 2013 from http://www.coram.org.uk/events/readmore/46/previous-events/5/1/2012/03/17

Kirby, P., Lanyon, C., Cronin, K., & Sinclair, R. (2003). *Building a culture of participation involving children and young people in policy, service planning, delivery and evaluation. Research report.* London: Department for Education and skills. Retrieved June 26, 2013 from http://healthissuescentre.org.au/images/uploads/resources/Building-a-culture-of-participation-handbook.pdf

Kreig, S. (2003). Ethical research with children: Practices and possibilities. *Australian Research in Early Childhood Education, 10*(1), 81–92.

Lancaster, Y. P., & Kirby, P. (2010). *Listening to young children: The reader.* London: Open University Press.

Leitch, R. (2008). Creatively researching children's narratives through image and drawings. In P. Thompson (Ed.), *Get the picture: Visual research with children and young people* (pp. 35–58). London: Routledge Falmer.

Lemon, N. (2008). Looking through the lens of a camera in the early childhood classroom. In J. Moss. (Ed.), *Research education: Visually-digitally-spatially* (pp. 21–52). Rotterdam, the Netherlands: Sense Publishers.

Lewis, M. (1993). Self-conscious emotions: Embarrassment, pride, shame and guilt. In M. Lewis & J.Haviland (Eds.), *Handbook of emotion* (pp. 563–573). New York, NY: Guilford Press.

MacNaughton, G. (2003a). *Shaping early childhood: Learners, curriculums and contexts.* Maidenhead: Open University Press.

MacNaughton, G. (2003b). Eclipsing voice in research with young children. *Australian Journal of Early Childhood Education, 28*(1), 36–42.

MacNaughton, G., Stratford, J., Agars, K., & Cook, P. (2006, December). *Under the radar, through the fog, into the future – Learner engagement through children's voices*. Paper presented at the conference of the Centre for Equity and Innovation in Early Childhood (CEIEC) Conference, The University of Melbourne, Melbourne, Australia.

Malaguzzi, L. (1998). History, ideas and basic philosophy. In C. Edwards, L. Gandini, & G. Foreman (Eds.), *The hundred languages of children*. Norwood, MA: Ablex.

Mauthner, M. (1997). Methodological aspects of collecting data from children: lessons from three research projects. *Children and Society, 11*, 16–28.

Mayall, B. (2000). Conversations with children: Working with generational issues. In P. Christensen & A. James (Eds.), *Research with children: Perspectives and practices* (pp. 120–135). London: Routledge Falmer.

Marshall, C. (2006). Tapping into passion and fury. *Journal of Research in Educational Leadership, 1*(1).

Marshall, F. (1997, September). Boost your baby's sense of self. *Parents*, 10–12.

Odom, S. L., & Strain, P. S. (2002). Evidence-Based practice in early intervention/Early childhood special education single-subject design research. *Journal of Early Intervention, 25*(2), 151–160.

O'Kane, C. (2000). The development or participatory techniques. Facilitating children's views about decisions which affect them. In P. Christensen & A. James (Eds.), *Research with children: Perspectives and practices* (pp. 120–135). London: Routledge Falmer.

Prior, M. A. & Niesz, T. (2013). Refugee children's adaptation to American early childhood classrooms: A narrative inquiry. *The Qualitative Report, 18*(39), 1–17.

Raban, B. (2000). *Just the beginning*. Report prepared for the Research and Evaluation Branch International Analysis and Evaluation Division, Department of Education, Training, and Youth Affairs, Canberra, ACT.

Ricœur, P. (1988). *Time and narrative* (Vol. 3). Chicago, IL: University of Chicago Press.

Robbins, J. (2003). The more he looked inside the more Piaget wasn't there: Why adopting a sociocultural perspective can help us see. *Journal of Early Childhood Education, 28*(2), 1–7.

Rodd, J. M. (1994) *Leadership in early childhood: The pathway to professionalism*. Sydney: Allen and Unwin.

Roskos, K., & Christie, J. (2001). Examining the play literacy interface: A critical review and future directions. *Journal of Early Childhood Literacy, 1*(1), 59–89.

Sumsion, J., & Goodfellow, J. (2012). Looking and listening-in: A methodological approach to generating insights into infants' experiences of early childhood education and care setting. *European Early Childhood Education Research Journal, 20*(3), 313–327.

Tayler, C. (2012). Learning in Australian early childhood education and care settings: Changing professional practice. *Education 3–13: International Journal of Primary Elementary and Early Years Education, 40*(1), 7–18.

Target, M., & Fonagy, P. (1996) Playing with reality: II. The development of psychic reality from a theoretical perspective. *International Journal of Psychoanalysis, 77*(3), 459–479.

Thomson, P. (2009). *Doing visual research with children and young people*. London: Routledge.

Trahar, S. (Ed.). (2011). *Learning and teaching narrative inquiry: Travelling in the borderlands*. Amsterdam, The Netherlands: John Benjamins Publishing Company.

Wong, S. S. (2003). A narrative inquiry into teaching of in-service kindergarten teachers: Implications for re-conceptualizing early childhood teacher education in Hong Kong. *Early Child Development and Care, 173*(1), 73–81.

Yelland, N. L. (2001). *Teaching and learning with information and communication technologies (ICT) for numeracy in the early childhood and primary years of schooling*. Melbourne: Department of Education, Training and Youth Affairs.

Narelle Lemon
La Trobe University

NARRATIVES FOR CHILDREN

INTRODUCTION

In many early childhood services for children, appropriating the paradigmatic of reasoning is already recognized in many activities such as categorization games and informational, expository texts (such as picture books about natural sciences) (Mantzicopoulos & Patrick, 2010). Research has also found that children who may not be the story teller can also learn narrative skills by being present, listening and becoming familiar with narrative genre from others (Rogoff et al., 2003). This means everyday activities that involve collective groups constitute important spaces for young children learning to narrate.

This chapter will discuss the intersection of narration with models of child development. There is a growing call in the literature (Mulvaney, 2011) for narration to grow within child development theories and theories of children's personality development. If it is the case that personality and development are fundamentally a narrative (Bruner, 2004), then a narrative perspective can inform the study of developmental processes. This new perspective has the potential to broaden the domains of cognitive, moral emotional and behavioural development. We can describe this as narratives for children.

This chapter will also discuss the role of the educator in supporting narration for young children. It will propose an enactive or phenomenological approach to social cognition, referred to as interaction theory. The chapter concludes with a consideration to *flip the concept* of narratives for children to *narratives for adults* (moving from a child development perceptions of narratives to a sense making perspective). This approach allows for socio-cultural understanding of children narratives and moves perceptions of children's narratives from developing to being highly competent in expressing their experiences and understanding of the world. While still acknowledging the intersection of developmental theories and narrative approaches, *narratives for adults* allows consideration of children's agency and competence.

THE INTERSECTION BETWEEN DEVELOPMENTAL THEORIES AND NARRATIVES APPROACHES

An early childhood centre is a busy place for children and adults. Each day is different with many unexpected conversations taking place. The daily lives of adults and children are filled with episodes. Episodes are described as short interactions of narrative communication. Children engage with adults about their events and happenings, hopes, dreams, fears and threats. While narrative events are fleeting moments, they provide situations for children to make sense of themselves and the world around them (Engel, 2006). Everyday narratives allow children an interactional forum for ordering, explaining and communicating their experiences (Ochs & Capps, 2001). Narrative also allow children to comment on their own development and show their current understandings to an adult. This is important because in most cultures children grown up surrounded by stories (Hutto, 2008). Narratives are therefore an important part in the daily lives of children and adults.

The current scientific interest in children's narratives has grown from research highlighting the connections between children's narratives and their overall development. Researchers have been able to explore how children learn to narrate and how narratives change depending on a child's age and development (Engel, 2006; Nicolopoulou & Richner, 2007). This has created a focus on child's language development and a child's own health and wellbeing. In such studies, narrative methods are used to support and enhance therapeutic goals and outcomes (Bennett, 2008).

The intersection of developmental theories and narrative approaches has also come from a moral perspective that considers children as subjects of value and individuals with rights (Greene & Hill, 2006). Children are now reviewed a competent contributors whose own experience is relevant to scientific research (Mayall, 2002). Furthermore, empirical research shows that when children are engaged appropriately in research, they are able to make significant contribution (Birbeck & Drummond, 2005; Einarsdottir, 2005).

By aligning narrative approaches with developmental theories, there are new ways of working for developmental intervention practices. Oppenheim (2006) argues that the divergent pathways of developmental competence and incompetence may substantially reflect differences in children's narrative representations. Some research suggests that children who life experiences have caused them to develop incomplete narratives may have poor psychological and behavioural attributes (Oppenheim, Nir, Warren & Ende, 1997). This implies that children's maladaptive behaviour may be able to be modified through narrative for children. Howard (1991, p. 194) describes this type of intervention as "story repair". By having interventions that aid children in developing appropriate narratives, language competency may be increased.

Another developmental intersection has been the emergence of attachment processes with narrative perspectives. Attachment has already been described in narrative terms (Nelson, 1999; Vaughn et al., 2006), helping improve insights into developmental processes. Bost et al. (2006) suggests the initial experiences children have with adult caregivers affects the relational processes of the child in subsequent romantic and caregiving relationships via the constructed narrations of life experiences with figures who service as attachment figures. Through caregiving experiences with families and educators, children construct narratives of the process of caregiving and start to discern their own and others' roles in social interactions.

From these studies we can see the importance of narrative to help foster the development of children.

INTERACTION THEORY

Narrative research often relies on verbal language through interaction. Children will use a range of narrative means to share, express and organize their experiences (Ahn & Filipenko, 2007; Engel, 2006; Puroila, Estola & Sryala, 2012). This type of multimodal expression from children requires sensitive listening from the adult's side. The role of the adult is to analyse and explore the narrative constructions of the child.

One theory useful for adults to understand is interaction theory. Interaction theory is described as a larger enactive or phenomenological approach to social cognition (Gallagher, 2012). Interaction theory (Gallagher, 2013, p. 5) relies "on developmental studies that demonstrate that our encounters with others are best characterized in terms of embodied interactions rather than the kind of mindreading defended by simulation theory or other theory-of-mind approaches".

There are different types of interactions children are involved in. These include (Gallagher, 2013, p. 5):

• Primary intersubjectivity (starting from birth) which involves the importance of the close company of others, imitation and dyadic interaction
• Secondary intersubjectivity (from before one year of age) which involves acting with others in pragmatic situations and learning by example.
• Communicative and narrative competences (developing for two to four years onwards) which involves sharing with adults and other children.

Communicative interactions are often shared by adults in early childhood settings who provide narrative experiences for young children, even before they can speak. This might include activities of reading to children and engaging the child in the story with actions and body contact. For example, the rhyme *Round and round the garden went the teddy bear* involves touching the child as different words are spoken. The rhyme is shown below.

• *Round and round the garden went the teddy bear* (educator traces a circle on the child's palm)
• *One Step, Two step* (educator imitates walking with their fingers on the child's arm)
• *Tickle under there* (educator imitates walking all the way of the child's arm)

In a recent research project, I collected a range of rhymes that involved spoken words and actions in an Australian kindergarten. Over a two week period, I sat in the back of an early childhood centre filming interactions that occurred. On average, two spoken/sung and actions rhymes were used an hour with individual children, while spoken/sung and actions rhymes were also used for whole class transitions. Examples of transition rhymes included:

There were five in the bed and the little one said roll over, roll over, so they all rolled over and one fell out. Five children are standing up making a rolling sign with their hands and then one children jumps away to represent falling out of bed.

Figure 1. There were five in the bed.

Five little ducks went out one day, over the hill and far away. Mother duck said quack, quack, quack. But only four little ducks came back. Five children are standing as the little ducks and showing various actions with their hands. Hands are used to say the duck going quack, quack, quack. A child then jumps away to represent four ducks.

Figure 2. Five little ducks.

Snail, snail, snail, snail go a round and round and round. Children all hold hands in a line. The teacher takes the hand of the first child and walks the children around in circles to show the shape of the snail's shell.

Figure 3. Snail, snail.

We are able to understand children's narratives in terms of their level of language acquisition. It is important that we understand the developmental story and how educators provide narrative experiences for children. With secondary intersubjectivity (from before one year of age), the educator will engage in a range of narrative practices to interact with the young child to provide examples of language and narrative practice. This includes conversations with children (even though they may not be able to provide a verbal response), reading with children and engaging them in active story telling with other children. At around 15–24 months children start to acquire language. The role of the educator is to incorporate these early utterances into narrative practices. At 18–24 months, children start to manifest ability for episodic and autobiographical memory (Howe, 2000). Young children begin to build the capacity for narrative practices. The role of the educator is to support these narrative practices. Research suggests that children at two years of age often work from short scripts rather than fully fledged narratives. Their self-narratives are often elicited by questions and prompts from adults (Howe, 2000; Nelson, 2009). The educator is therefore responsible for questioning and prompting children to tell and retell their own stories. An example below is shared of an educator emerging in questioning and prompting with a young child:

Child:	*Me and mommy went to the park.*
Teacher:	*Why did you go to the park?*
Child:	*Swings and the slides and the blocks and the ladder and the whirly. But I hurt!*
Teacher:	*What happened at the park?*
Child:	*I hurt on the block. My knee hit.*

In this example the child is describing an event that the child experienced. Through questioning, the child was able to build on their story to allow the teacher to witness more details.

In the early study mentioned about rhymes used in an early childhood setting, various questioning was created after the event. For example, one child was interested to know more about the missing ducks:

Child:	*If ducks take phone they won't be lost.*
Teacher:	*Why won't they be lost?*

Child: *The phone tells you where to go. The ducks could ring each other.*
Teacher: *So should all the ducks have a phone?*
Child: *Yes—Mummy duck needs to buy more phones. Then no-one lost. If*
              they can't find they ring.

Child puts their hand (in the form of a phone) to their ear and begins talking to mother duck.

In the above example we also begin to see the emergence of digital technology in the child's life. We are shown that the child knows that phones can also be used to help with directions besides making contact with people. The child also shows evidence of problem solving the concept of being 'lost' in this short interaction.

From two to four years of age, children start to fine-tune their narrative practices through further language and memory development. Children in this age range will sometimes 'appropriate' someone else's story as their own (Nelson, 2003). Children have the capability to produce logically and sequentially organized scenes that can be recalled independently (Nelson & Fivush, 2004). This stems largely from the development of an autobiographical memory system that emerges after infancy. After four years of age children start to represent the views of others in their narratives, showing what they know and others know about events (Nelson, 1993; Perner, 1992). With an understanding that others have intentions and goals that are different from the child themselves, there is "increased motivation to discern the motivations and likely behaviours of others in social scenarios and narration provides the means to do so" (Mulvaney, 2011, p. 1156). Narrative practice is therefore understood as tools by which human beings organize their personal experiences (Bruner, 1990; Engel, 2006). In this context, it allows young children to demonstrate understandings about their own development.

CREATING SPACES FOR CHILDREN'S NARRATIVE

Questions and prompts are one tool educators use to engage children in narratives. It is important however for the educator to also have an understanding of physical responses. For example, when a child responds to a direct question from an educator, the physical response may say more than words. Through questions, the educator will be able to direct young children's attention towards what they consider worth telling (Aukrust, 1996; Ødegaard, 2006). The educator must be sensitive of the multimodal aspects of narrative, including nonverbal cues from body language, facial cues, emotional expressions and actions (Ahn & Filipenko, 2007; Bamberg & Georgakopoulou, 2008; Estola, Farquhar & Puroila, 2013).

Narratives are also told to audiences by young children—either real or imagined. The role of the audience ranges from a passive listener to an active co-teller (Ochs & Capps, 2001; Viljamaa, 2010). It is therefore important that adults make themselves available for children's narratives. In some early childhood research, adults in a day care context have developed a passive role in which they leave children to choose their activities and do not engage in interaction with the children (Kalliala, 2008; Puroila, 2002). In these instances, children lose the opportunity to share their experiences, while adults lose the opportunities to gain insights into the children's experiences and ways of understanding the world. Educators sometimes under-utilize the rich pedagogical potential of narratives (Tsai, 2007). Puriola, Estola and Sryala (2012, p. 203) suggest that "staff members should become aware of the power of narratives in order to develop the pedagogical culture in day care centres favourable to children's everyday narratives". As one staff member in their study commented (Puriola, Estola & Sryala, 2012, p. 203), "Oh, these children surely have so much to tell. I wonder why I haven't listened to them more".

There are two important elements to develop a space for children's narrative in early childhood settings. These elements help develop a pedagogical environment that supports and enhances young children's every narratives. The first element is providing space for narratives. Space for narrating means both physical space, space in timetabling and also space for valuing children's expressions. Children need to have space (both ideological and moral) in their daily lives for spontaneous narratives.

The second element is a receptive educator is actively engaged in the daily lives of the children. This means that the educator know the right time when to co-construct narratives with young children and to also allow other times for children to co-construct meaning with one another.

The receptive educator has the opportunity to affect the content of narrative by aiding children in extracting appropriate and relevant features of the narrative. Adults therefore have a role of aiding children to construct narratives with a developmental process so that children come to rely less on partners in the construction of their narratives.

For some educators this requires a change in perception and the daily running of their routines. I recently collected data from an educator in a kindergarten who wanted to engage in narrative research. I had been working with her to think about making spaces for narratives and the importance of being a receptive educator. Over a period time we worked on both concepts. We would meet regularly to discuss the data she was collecting from the children's narratives. Towards the end of the research project, she began talking about the importance of narrative in her own teaching life. The teacher began to realise the importance of not only listening to the children's narratives, but also her own personal narrative of transformation. She began to write down her thoughts and then discuss them with me in an interview. We decided to conduct an investigation into her ideas. Over five interviews we collected her personal story of experience of her teaching transformation. We would find a theme and then revisit the theme in the next interview. Sometimes the story would be retold to provide new meaning and understanding. Below is an insert from her personal narrative:

Initially I found it really difficult to allow space and time for narratives. We had so much to get through each day so the children would become school ready.

I had so many checklists to do and I had to undertake numerous observations of their learning and development. I decided to take a step back after one child told me I didn't listen to them. I realised my planning and also my pedagogical approach needed to change. We created a meeting circle where I encouraged the children to discuss when they felt they weren't being listened to and when they wanted to share their experiences. The majority of young children did not enjoy the rule to eat lunch silently. The children suggested they would like to talk to me and to one another. They said that they often spoke at home during meal times and didn't understand why they had to be quiet. Originally the quiet rule was introduced so the children would eat all of the food. I soon realised the children were missing out on valuable opportunities for creating their own narratives. We also look at other times in the day where the children and myself could share more interactions, rather than me just sitting back and observing the children around work stations all the time. I now find that I am more engaged and the children are also keen to share stories. I feel like they have been given opportunities to improve their communication and language skills. I am also exploring narrative story cards to help the children further. I want to reflect further on my practice with the children's help to see how we can allow even more opportunities for narrative telling.

We see from the above vignette the importance of rethinking practice and daily routines in a kindergarten from the teacher's perspective. When the educator was able to move towards become a receptive educator, she was able to transform her own thinking about children's narratives.

The personal narrative also highlights the importance of reflective practice for professionals working with young children. By exploring self-narratives, professionals are also able to understand their own ways of working with young children when engaging with narratives.

FUTURE RESEARCH

While there is much potential for the intersection of narrative perspectives with developmental perspectives, there is still a lack of empirical base research to support this combination (Bruner, 2004; Habermas & Bluck, 2000; Mulvaney, 2011). The narrative perspective has potentially broad implications for developmental theories but requires additional types of research to fully exploit its potential. This includes the development of tools that incorporate narrative and developmental perspectives that provide rigorous qualitative assessments. Such tools could be used to model changes in the narrative structure of children's stories over time and explore personalities for early intervention in narrative development. Narratives used in this way also allows the exploration of contemporary themes in early childhood including digital technology, gender, democracy, ethnicity and issues of place.

Future research is also needed that understands the importance of children as capable and confident beings within developmental theories. Rather than traditional perspectives of developing skills, new ways of understanding children as already competent and able to show us their understanding of the world is needed. While this might seem contradictory to developmental theories in which a child is always 'developing', development could also be seen in terms of loss or what the child is 'losing' as the move towards adult constructed concepts of narratives and stories. If the loss is creativity in innovation for example, perhaps early intervention is necessary to ensure that this personality characteristic can be supported beyond early childhood.

Incorporating children of all ages into narrative research is also needed. Often in children's research, children who are in the preverbal phase of development are often excluded because they do not fit traditional models of creating a well-formed narrative. Rather than treating children as developing narrators, research must consider developing new ways of thinking about children as competent narratives who are able to communicate their experiences. Instead of pre-determined definitions of narratives, very young children can show narration in their own way. Rather than children developing narrative skills, children are competent in their own story telling and choose what they want to show an adult.

FLIPPING THE CONCEPT—NARRATIVES FOR ADULTS

While this chapter has largely focused on children as developing narrative skills and language, there is another way to consider children's narrative making. Instead of a focus on 'narratives for children', we can flip the term by exploring 'narratives for adults'. By viewing from a different perspective, we are able to share contemporary perspectives of narrative. This will be explained in more detail below by examining closer links between human experience and narrative.

The intersection is also based on the scientific potential of exploring children's narratives to show relationships between human experience and narrative. Narrative research is often inspired by a view of human experience that is based on John's Dewey's pragmatic philosophy (Clandinin, 2006). Children's experiences in their everyday life are represented in the form of narratives and stories (Riessman, 1993). Starting from this point of view, narratives allow researchers insights in the experience of a child's world. In a developmental sense, it also represents the current state of the child's development by showing representation of the child level of understanding. The child is considered competent and capable in displaying how they come to know and understand the world around them. Children choose how they would like to communicate this meaning to adults.

The process of narration is also a culture-specific process that can represent a potential framework for enhancing contextualist theories of development (Bruner, 1990; Singer, 2004). Narrative can bridge cultural modes of thinking and the ways in which children come to reasons and behave in culture-specific ways. In this way, children's thinking reflects the modes of thinking of those who collectively make up a particular cultural group in which the children collaborates. Contemporary issues of place become important in analysis. The concept of place becomes a key features in how children interact and communicate with each other.

The majority of narrative research with children is language oriented. The majority of studies on children and narratives focus on the comprehension of stories (read and told) and levels of competency. Few studies have actually studied the spontaneous everyday narratives created by children themselves (Ahn & Filipenko; Ochs & Capps, 2001). The concept of a narrative in many studies relies on a method of stories being verbally articulated, casually connected sequences in a goal-directed activity, appearing as criteria of a well-formed narrative (Nicolopoulou, 2008).

As an adult, we want stories to proceed in a linear and chronological way. The Aristotelian notion of a good narrative is to have a clear beginning, middle and end (Hyvärinen Hyden, Saarenheimo & Tamboukou, 2010). If we place this perspective of a 'good narrative' for young children, we will also view their stories as deficits. In a recent research project, children's stories were often two to four words in length. For example, one child stated *Dog hurt*. From some adult's perspectives this could be viewed as an incomplete narrative without further information about the story.

Nicolopoulou (2008) argues that when children's stories to not match adult perceptions of a good story they are analysed in a negative way. For this reason, we can argue that 'narratives' have not been at the centre of a researcher's interest. As Flewitt (2005) argues, the current focus on young children is with spoken interaction, while the diversity of ways of children's meaning-making is largely ignored. Young children are perceived as becoming story tellers and not viewed as competent and capable organisers of their own communication. In the above example of *Dog hurt* the child is able to show us their understanding about an injured dog they had seen walking to the childcare centre. The child was also able to show usage of word order and meaning. The child could have stated *Hurt dog* which may have implied a different meaning to the child's meaning. Along with the child's spoken words, the child acted out with gestures the story, providing an alternate way of communicating the bigger narrative.

We can flip this perception of children's narratives as deficit in structure by having the concept of 'narrative for adults'. In this way, all children (including pre-verbal) are considered active and capable communicators of their own experiences. Children have their own views and conceptions of stories and narratives that they can choose to communicate in a variety of ways to adults. While children can have words, actions and emotional expressions, silence and non-acting (e.g., resisting) can also serve as powerful tools of narration (Puroila, Estol & Syrjala, 2012).

Children also have fragmented stories in which many things can occur at the same children. Children will move back and forth in their actions and talk. They may also launch narratives without clear signs of where they may lead (Ochs & Capps, 2001). Children do not have to follow adult perspectives of an Aristotelian narrative. Rather children are individuals in their own rights who choose how and what they communicate to adults. The narrative that a child creates and shares therefore becomes available to adults, allowing small windows into the child's world. Children give their *narratives for adults.*

Interestingly some research shows that as children leave early childhood settings, their narratives lose unique richness. Narratives begin to resemble the narratives of adults by becoming more complete and conventional at the expense of being personal, creative and vivid (Engel, 2006). It is vital for us to consider the importance of children as capable story tellers.

One study that has approached narratives from a children's perspective was conducted by Puroila, Estola and Syrjala (2013). They noted that when the approach is flipped there is an opportunity to understand that children's everyday narrative contain untapped pedagogical potential in an early childhood context. Puroila, Estola and Syrjala (2013, p. 203) suggested that:

> ...narratives involve ethical and moral questions about children's voices, their right to express themselves, and to be listened to and heard. A narrative is a meeting place in which an individual child encounters the community consisting of peers and adults. Through narratives, children build relationships, create a sense of belonging, collaborate, tell and listen, face and solve problems, share experiences, and continually construct their worldview and identity.

Narratives provide important windows into the lives of children. By understanding the role of daily narratives in the lives of children, we can use this approach to collect and document the child's understanding and learning.

LIMITATIONS

While it is important to realize the potential of narratives for young children, we must also visit the limitations and challenges when interpreting narratives in terms of children's experiences. Although educators may be offered insight into children's lives, there is a need for educators not to simplify the interpretation of these stories. As an adult, we must acknowledge that while we can prompt and be involved in children's narrations, we do not have unfettered access to children's experiences. We also cannot generalize children. Complexities in interpretation can includes variations in children's age, early childhood settings and pedagogy towards narrative practice. From children's narrative, it is therefore difficult to provide international comparison or a generalized conclusion.

Another limitation is that in accordance with narrative scholars, it is also acknowledged that researchers and educators do not have direct access to human experience. Rather it is only a child's reported experience. The inaccessibility is more evident with pre-verbal children who are unable to report their experiences. However, some contemporary research on children's experiences also emphasises the symbolic as well as socially mediated and shared nature of experience (Greene & Hill, 2006).

CONCLUSION

When discussing narratives for children, it is important to also consider the concept of narratives for adults. This chapter has discussed the intersection between developmental theories and narrative research. It has provided insight into respecting children's narratives, as well as highlighting the role of the educator and researcher. Some of the key themes explored were digital technology, ableness and place.

What is important to remember is that early childhood settings offer opportunities to tap into new ways of thinking about children. While much attention has been paid to children's language development through narrative, less attention has been paid to children's spontaneous narratives in their everyday lives in early childhood settings. Greater awareness and understanding is needed for the widespread importance of narrative as a sense-making form for young children (Bamberg, 2007; Bruner, 1990, 2002; Kamberelis, 1999; Ochs & Capps, 2001; van Oers, 2003; and Tomasello, 1999). The next chapter will move beyond the concept of narrative for children to explore the concept of narratives with children. Narratives with children explains the concept of co-construction of narratives between the child and educator. Contemporary themes of digital meaning-making and intersections with popular children's culture will be explored.

REFERENCES

Ahn, J., & Filipenko, M. (2007). Narrative, imaginary play, art, and self: Intersecting worlds. *Early Childhood Education Journal, 34*, 279–289.
Aukrust, V. G. (2005). *Tidlig språkstimulering og livslang læring: En kunnskapsoversikt* [Early literacy intervention and lifelong learning: A research overview]. Norway: Norwegian Department of Knowledge.
Bamberg, M. G. W. (Ed.). (2007). *Narrative: State of the art.* Amsterdam: John Benjamins.
Bamberg, M., & Georgakopoulou, A. (2008). Small stories as a new perspective in narrative and identity analysis. *Text & Talk, 28*, 377–396.
Bennett, L. (2008). Narrative methods and children: Theoretical explanations and practical issues. *Journal of Child and Adolescent Psychiatric Nursing, 21*, 13–23.
Birbeck, D., & Drummond, M. (2005). Interviewing, and listening to the voices of, very young children on body image and perceptions of self. *Early Child Development and Care, 175*, 579–596. doi: 10.1080/03004430500131379
Bost, K. K., Shin, N., McBride, B. A., Brown, G. L., Vaughn, B. E., Coppola, G., & Korth, B. (2006). Maternal secure base scripts, children's attachment security, and mother–child narrative styles. *Attachment & Human Development, 8*, 241–260.
Bruner, J. (1990). *Acts of meaning.* Cambridge, MA: Harvard University Press.
Bruner, J. (2004). Life as narrative. *Social Research, 71*, 691–710.
Bruner, J. S. (2002). *Making stories: Law, literature, life.* Cambridge, MA: Harvard University Press.
Clandinin, D. J. (2006). Narrative inquiry: A methodology for studying lived experience. *Research Studies in Music Education, 27*, 44–54.
Engel, S. (2006). Narrative analysis of children's experience. In S. Greene & D. Hogan (Eds.), *Researching children's experience: Approaches and methods* (pp. 199–216). London: Sage.
Einarsdottir, J. (2005). Playschool in pictures: Children's photographs as research methods. *Early Child Development and Care, 175*, 523–541.
Estola, E., Farquar, S., & Puroila, A. M. (2013). Well-being narratives and young children. *Educational Philosophy and Theory*, 1–13. Retrieved from http://dx.doi.org/10.1080/00131857.2013.785922

Flewitt, R. (2005). Is every child's voice heard? Researching the different ways 3-year-old children communicate and make meaning at home and in pre-school playgroup. *Early Years, 25*, 207–222. doi: 10.1080/09575140500251558

Gallagher, S. (2013). An education in narratives. *Educational Philosophy and Theory, 46*(6), 600–609. doi: 10.1080/00131857.2013.779213

Gallagher, S. (2012). In defense of phenomenological approaches to social cognition: Interacting with the critics. *Review of Philosophy and Psychology, 3*, 187–212.

Greene, S., & Hill, M. (2006). Researching children's experience: Methods and methodological issues. In S. Greene & D. Hogan (Eds.), *Researching children's experience: Approaches and methods* (pp. 1–21). London: Sage.

Habermas, T., & Bluck, S. (2000). Getting a life: The emergence of the life story in adolescence. *Psychological Bulletin, 126*, 748–769.

Howard, G. S. (1991). Culture tales: A narrative approach to thinking, cross-cultural psychology, and psychotherapy. *American Psychologist, 46*, 187–197.

Howe, M. L. (2000). *The fate of early memories: Developmental science and the retention of childhood experiences.* Cambridge, MA: MIT Press.

Hutto, D. D. (2008). *Folk psychological narratives: The socio-cultural basis of understanding reasons.* Cambridge, MA: MIT Press.

Hyvärinen, M., Hydén, L.-C., Saarenheimo, M., & Tamboukou, M. (2010). Beyond narrative coherence: An introduction. In M. Hyvärinen, L.-C. Hydén, M. Saarenheimo, & M. Tamboukou (Eds.), *Beyond narrative coherence* (pp. 1–15). Amsterdam: John Benjamins.

Kamberelis, G. (1999). Genre development and learning: Children writing stories, science reports, and poems. *Research in the Teaching of English, 33*(4), 403–460.

Kalliala, M. (2008). *Kato mua! Kohtaako aikuinen lapsen päiväkodissa?* [Look at me! Does the adult encounter the child at a day care center?]. Helsinki: Gaudeamus.

Mantzicopoulos, P., & Patrick, H. (2010). The seesaw is a machine that goes up and down: Young children's narrative responses to science-related informational text. *Early Education and Development, 21*(3), 412–444.

Mayall, B. (2002) *Towards a sociology for childhood: Thinking from children's lives.* Maidenhead: Open University Press.

Mulvaney, M. K. (2011) Narrative processes across childhood. *Early Child Development and Care, 181*(9),1153–1161.

Nelson, K. (2009). Narrative practices and folk psychology: A perspective from developmental psychology. *Journal of Consciousness Studies, 16*, 69–93.

Nelson, K. (2003). Narrative and the emergence of a consciousness of self. In G. D. Fireman, T. E. J. McVay, & O. Flanagan (Eds.), *Narrative and consciousness* (pp. 17–36). Oxford: Oxford University Press.

Nelson, K. (1999). Event representations, narrative development, and internal working models. *Attachment & Human Development, 1*, 239–252.

Nelson, K. (1993). The psychological and social origins of autobiographical memory. *Psychological Science, 4*, 7–14.

Nelson, K., & Fivush, R. (2004). The emergence of autobiographical memory: A social cultural developmental model. *Psychological Review, 111*, 486–511.

Nicolopoulou, A. (2008). The elementary forms of narrative coherence in young children's storytelling. *Narrative Inquiry, 18*, 299–325. doi: 10.1075/ni.18.1.07nic

Nicolopoulou, A., & Reichner, E. S. (2007). From actors to agents to persons: The development of character representation in young children's narratives. *Child Development, 78*, 412–429.

Ochs, E., & Caps, L. (2001). *Living narratives.* Cambridge, MA: Harvard University Press.

Oppenheim, D. (2006). Child, parent, and parent–child emotion narratives: Implications for developmental psychopathology. *Developmental and Psychopathology, 18*, 771–790.

Oppenheim, D., Nir, A., Warren, S., & Emde, R. N. (1997). Emotion regulation in mother–child narrative co-construction: Associations with children's narratives and adaptation. *Developmental Psychology, 33*, 284–294.

Perner, J. (1992). Grasping the concept of representation: Its impact on 4-year-olds' theory of mind and beyond. *Human Development, 35*, 146–155.

Pramling, N., & Ødegaard, E. E. (2011). Learning to narrate: Appropriating a cultural mould for sense-making and communication. In N. Pramling & I. Pramling Samuelsson (Eds.), *Educational encounters: Nordic studies in early childhood didactics* (pp. 15–35). Dordrecht, the Netherlands: Springer.

Puroila, A.-M. (2002). *Kohtaamisia päiväkotiarjessa – Kehysanalyyttinen näkökulma varhaiskasvatustyöhön* [Encounters in day care centres – A frame analysis of early childhood work]. Oulu: University of Oulu.

Puroila, A.-M., Estola, E., & Syrjälä, L. (2012). Does Santa exist? Children's everyday narratives as dynamic meeting places in a day care centre context. *Early Child Development and Care, 182*, 191–206.

Riessman, C. K. (1993). *Narrative analysis*. Thousand Oaks, CA: Sage.

Rogoff, B., Paradise, R., Mejía Arauz, R., Correa-Cháves, M., & Angelillo, C. (2003). Firsthand learning through intent participation. *Annual Review of Psychology, 54*, 175–203.

Singer, J. A. (2004). Narrative identity and meaning making across the adult lifespan: An introduction. *Journal of Personality, 72*, 437–459.

Tomasello, M. (1999). *The cultural origins of human cognition*. Cambridge, MA: Harvard University Press.

Tsai, M.-L. (2007). Understanding young children's personal narratives. In D. J. Clandinin (Ed.), *Narrative inquiry: Mapping a methodology* (pp. 461–488). Thousand Oaks, CA: Sage.

van Oers, B. (2003). Multiple narratives of childhood: Tools for the improvement of early childhood education. In B. van Oers (Ed.), *Narratives of childhood: Theoretical and practical explorations for the innovation of early childhood education* (pp. 9–26). Amsterdam: VU University Press.

Vaughn, B. E., Waters, H. S., Coppola, G., Cassidy, J., Bost, K. K., & Verissimo, M. (Eds.). (2006). Script-like attachment representations and behavior in families and across cultures [Special issue]. *Attachment & Human Development, 8*(3), 179–184.

Viljamaa, E. (2010). Block story: Listening to child's narrating at home. In E.-L. Kronqvist & P. Hyvönen (Eds.), *Insights and outlouds: Childhood research in the North* (pp. 173–184). Oulu: University of Oulu.

Ødegaard, E. E. (2006). What's worth talking about? Meaning-making in toddler-initiated conarratives in preschool. *Early Years, 26*(1), 79–92.

Susanne Garvis
University of Gothenburg

CHAPTER 5

NARRATIVE RESEARCH WITH CHILDREN

INTRODUCTION

This chapter will examine children's narrative meaning-making as a co-constructional process. Narrative meaning-making is seen as closely interwoven with the human, material, ideological and cultural context in which children take part. The chapter will outline a dialogical perspective on children's narratives as co-construction. It will suggest ways that teacher educators and researchers can study how children and teachers share and negotiate meaning and thereby how and with what kind of issues and experiences children bring in and become a participant of a wider cultural community.

Narrative practice is considered a process of collaborative meaning-making. Studied in the context of early childhood institutions, narrative practice is considered, in one form or another, as co-narrative. Narrative practice embraces the terms *story* and *story telling*. The story concept will more specifically refer to provoked stories as in *story table activities* in kindergarten. We would suggest that it is possible, from a very early age to elicit, invite, listen and support children's utterances (oral, gesture, body) in a narrative research approach that considers narratives as co-constructions.

KNOWLEDGE FROM A CO-NARRATIVE APPROACH

A co-narrative approach is suitable for studies when we want to understand what content very young children bring to early childhood settings and how children co-construct curriculum with teachers. It is also suitable for studies where the research interest lies in how the child make sense of local and global culture and how children are shaped as individuals and how they participate in the formation of the peer culture and the everyday curriculum.

Co-narrative practice is considered a process of collaborative meaning-making. It is a way of knowing and communicating experiences, organizing a plot temporally and spatially or connecting utterances, as well as gestures, performance and acting into episodic meaning.

We need to develop age-appropriate research approaches for the youngest children. In multicultural societies, culture-sensitive research approaches are important in order to understand children in a broad sense. Research approaches that consider cultural varieties, historical and ideological routes in which children participate as parts of families and communities, can help us understand more of how kindergarten and society at large conditions children's meaning-making, identity processes and learning.

High quality services for the under three demand insights in and knowledge about children's meaning-making and communication of perspectives. Such an approach could give understandings of what kind of issues are important for the youngest from their perspective: What is worth telling and talking about?

Early childhood teachers and staff will condition children's processes of shaping cultural and personal identity by how they support children, who they support and when they support narratives. One could also say *if* they support narrative initiatives from children or *if* they take the initiative to tell and invite children to co-construct experiences. Whether they do or do not support young children's initiatives to tell, or invite children into reconstruction to tell or ignore this way of being and communicating makes a difference in children's lives.

New knowledge about how early childhood institutional setting conditions children's sense of belonging, their cultural shaping, meaning-making and learning could derive from questions like:

- What issues are supported by adults/peers?
- How do the modes of conversation give value to certain ways of communication?

If and how narratives are constructed will also condition children's sense and modes of lived democracy. Are their initiatives taken up and acted upon? An important question for researching democratic issues are:

- Are young children given the opportunity to participate in dialogical cultural practices?
- Do the staff have time, knowledge and cultures for co-narrating with young children and follow up on children's utterances?

In late modernity globalization of culture raises many questions of interest for high quality practice with children. Cultural heroes and antiheroes are presented for children through multimedia and so on. It is of pedagogical and research interest to know more about what inspires children. How do small children deal with experiences from real, virtual and media life? What kind of heroes are made available for them in everyday life? What do children do with these heroes and antiheroes?

Children's oral stories, co-narratives as well as narrative practice in fiction play, drawings and digital collages give rich opportunities for studying narrative practice as a site for cultural practice. Children's use of texts, stories, fairy tales, films, and so on, that are made available to them are studied within the framework of ethnography and narrative analysis (Ødegaard, 2011a)

NARRATIVE RESEARCH AS A DIALOGICAL CO-CONSTRUCTION

According to Catherine Kohler Riessman, dialogic analysis is concerned with how narratives are co-produced in a complex choreography, in spaces between teller and listener, speaker and setting, text and reader, history and culture (Riessman 2008, p. 105). Characteristic of this kind of analysis is that the researcher is actively present in the text and that the context is considered to be important. With reference to Erving Goffman, Riessman adds importance to the performative act, when analysing identity. Bodily forms of communication come into play. Such a consideration is convenient when looking for characters that children take up when telling and playing stories. Hence, the term narrative here refers to a general way of knowing and communicating experiences, organizing a plot temporally and spatially, or connecting utterances and act into meaning.

The attempt to conceptualize children's narratives for the purpose of studying conditions for children's meaning making and cultural shaping where laid out as operating in a web of structural, contextual relationships (Ødegaard, 2011b). The interest is obviously *not* developmental, rather it lies in studying children's narratives as cultural practice. Conditions like cultural artefacts, books, theatre, personal stories, legends and videogames are made available by teachers' (and researchers') ideologies and practice and will constitute and shape institutional practice that can be part of the narrative process.

Bakhtin's philosophical contribution, dialogism, gives important insight into understanding the dynamics of narrative practice in early childhood institutions. These practices are to be understood as heteroglossic. Bakhtin puts it like this:

> At any given time, in any given place, there will be a set of conditions – social, historical, meteorological, physiological – that will insure that a word uttered in that place and at that time will have a meaning different than it would have under any other conditions; all utterances are heteroglot in that they are functions of a matrix of forces practically impossible to recoup, and therefore impossible to resolve. (Bakhtin, 1981, p. 428)

Even though Bakhtin neither empirically dealt with early childhood studies, nor was concerned with children's narratives, his dialogic approach is productive in studies of children's narrative meaning-making practices. Such an approach allows studies of both form and content—narratives can be seen as generating themes and meaning-making in contexts. Within this scope, meaning-making practices are seen as becoming and emerging in dynamic social interaction. A subject can speak by using existing artefacts. In a dialogic perspective, informed by Bakhtin, every text will include many voices, hidden discourses, politics, ideologies and values. Any utterance will be saturated by meanings coming from earlier users. "The word in language is half someone else's" (Bakhtin 1981, p. 293). In this theoretical framework, children's narratives are not considered as coming from the inner soul, rather as emerging from a dialogic process (Ødegaard, 2007, 2011c).

Consequently narratives are viewed as a speech and act genre, through which young children participate in cultural activities. At the same time as they use narrative genre to shape inner meaning, they are exposed to narratives and thereby participate in a web of structural and relational conditions (Bruner, 1990; Hirschkop & Shepherd, 2001; Junefelt, 2009). Children are, implicitly as well as explicitly, exposed to cultural artefacts like books, films, toys, such as, for example, spin-off products from films made for children, all of which are possible to study in the microcosm of co-narrative practice in an early childhood setting. Such artefacts are the stuff children take up when creating their own stories. Texts made available to children are re-circulated in their modes of action and speech, as culturally formative practices.

In Bakhtinian terms, children's narratives are viewed as hybrids, "a multiplicity of social voices and a wide variety of their links and inter relationships" (Bakhtin, 1981, p. 263). In dialogism, meaning-making is considered a shared activity. Genres and words in use arise from the social practices in a given community, as also pointed out by Mika Lähteenmäki (Lähteenmäki, 2004).

UNDERSTANDING MEANING IN CONTEXT

Early childhood practice is, as we have stated throughout this book, fundamentally a relational pedagogical practice. Personal experience and local knowledge include a wide space for local judgment in particular situations and are seen as crucial. Borders between self and other are explored when telling, listening, picking up on others utterances and gestures and retelling is going on. A child could be put in situations where decentration and understanding others utterances is going on in the process of telling and listening.

A more specific analysis of the hybrid nature of children's narratives can be allowed by taking on board the concept of intertextuality (Kristeva, 1967, translated in 1980). Intertextuality describes the practice of making connections between texts, as pointed out by Bakhtin.

A superficial analysis of how children's narratives belong to other texts was done to a sample narrative, most of them transcribed from video observation, and some written down from situations of story making with children where the material was grounded in a study of what kind of cultural heroes and anti-heroes inspires children in fictionate narratives. The study could give insight into what cultural resources are found in children's co-narratives. This, in turn, could point to what kind of cultural resources are made available for children in any particular local context.

In the analysis, types of characters/protagonists that the children brought into their fiction narratives were identified and what kind of cultural patterns, modes and aesthetics were found in the narratives.

The overview exposes how children's narrative meaning-making in kindergartens in Norway are related to popular media from the Scandinavian and Anglo-American hemisphere. From the overview, we can see that children make meaning with physically powerful characters. Taking a socio-epistemological glance, it could be noticed that the characters are mostly male and animals are often used to symbolize attack or aggression. Two girls' references to Astrid Lindgren's stories of *Pippi Longstocking* seem to be an exception when it comes to gender. We examine the example of exception, that came into being during a provoked story telling session.

Table 2. Overview of children's co-narratives and relation to texts and contexts

Protagonists	Intertext	Available artefact in kindergarten	Author of intertext	Cultural context
Captain Sabertooth	Captain Sabertooth	Books, CDs, imaginary use of artefact	Terje Formoe	Scandinavian/ American
Captain Hook	Peter Pan	Imaginary use of artefact	Originally Sir James Matthew Barrie	European/ American
Captain Blackbill	Kaptein Sortebill	Song	Torbjørn Egner	Norwegian (American)
Father Christmas	Traditional	Local kindergarten stories, kindergarten celebration	Multiple origins, folklore	European/ American/ Global
Pippi Longstocking	Pippi Longstocking	Books	Astrid Lindgren	Scandinavian
Police	Media, everyday life	Miniature toy, blue shirt for role play	Multiple	Scandinavian/ American
Person in Star Wars	Star Wars film	Imaginary use of artefacts	George Lucas	
Indians	Traditional	Books, excursion to museum	Multiple	American
Lion	Lion King, books of wild animal	Books, miniature toy	Multiple	American and other
Shark	Various science literature	Books, internet, miniature toy	Multiple	Australian/ American

CREATING A PIPPI LONGSTOCKING STORY

At the spring festival, the children came to kindergarten dressed in various costumes. While waiting for the meal and peak event, it was time for drawing and story telling. We sat down at the story table, Maia and Rikke, both four years of age and me (Elin), a visiting researcher, with an inviting narrative approach. At the table were pencils and papers, my story-writing book and a pen. Around us were other children in the kindergarten group, most of them sitting down drawing, some children are playing with Lego bricks in a corner. Last week, when I was there, we followed the same routine. I invited them to a story telling session. We sat down. I wrote down the story verbatim. Now it was time to do it again. Both of them were eager to draw and tell when getting an invitation. Both of the girls were dressed in *Pippi Longstocking* costumes.

Maia:	*Pippi Longstocking can see a ship, then she can put people on fire,then they will die. [Pause, while both of them are drawing].*
Elin:	*Oh, what happened next?*
Maia:	*Then she said oops! Afterwards, Pippi should put the fire out. [Pause, while drawing].*
Elin:	*Are there more people there?*
Maia:	*Everyone living in Bergen were there, they were very happy when she put the fire out.*
Rikke:	*The ship is called Sleeping Beauty, white and yellow. The children were dead, but they woke up again. Maia and Rikke, they survived, they didn't die. They just ran away from the fire, they didn't burn, their house burnt down. Then they ran to somebody else.*
Maia:	*They ran to Pippi Longstocking. Her house was not on fire. They ran to the house that couldn't burn and that was Maia's house. Her mother and father were at home. They ran from the rain. We had so strong arms, we were Pippi Longstocking. We could save them from the fire.*

Analysing narrative practice as dialogic challenges the notion that it is individuals that tell rational and coherent stories about themselves to each other. This co-narrative about *Pippi Longstocking* and the fire was constructed cooperatively by the two girls and me. The fact that this was happening at the spring festival day, and that both of the girls were dressed with *Pippi Longstocking* costumes from a toy shop carried obvious signs and modes for the girls when being invited to tell a story.

It is Maia that introduces the theme and the character. She chooses *Pippi Longstocking* as the protagonist of her story. The first line: *Pippi Longstocking can see a ship, then she can put people on fire, then they will die,* set a violent and dramatic scene. This line is also in fact a three line story in an Aristotle's sense, with an introduction with a protagonist, a crucial incident and a consequence as an end. It is me, the researcher, that takes the lead to extend the story, and to include more than one author, when I say, *Oh, what happened next?* It is Maia who continues, *Then she said oops! Afterwards, Pippi should put the fire out.* Maia is first telling about a forceful *Pippi* that can put people on fire, *Pippi* here is a bad character. In the next line however, she is a hero, who can rescue people. Maia is playing out *Pippi* as a character that at first is being bad, and then being good. Responding to the opportunity to extend her narrative, she also changes her speech plan. Maia uses the *Pippi* character in a new thematic setting. Later, it is me again that conditions an extension of the story when saying, *Are there more people there?* This utterance gives a direction for what can come next. Maia continues: *Everyone living in Bergen was there, they were very happy when she put the fire out.* Now it seems that Rikke is becoming engaged in the narration process—she continues: *The ship is called Sleeping Beauty, white and yellow. The children were dead, but they woke up again. Maia and Rikke, they survived, they didn't die. They just ran away from the fire, they didn't burn, their house burnt down. Then they ran to somebody else.* She introduces another intertext, the fairy tale and Disney film, *Sleeping Beauty*, as the name of the ship. She introduces more to the story, themselves—Maia and Rikke. She refers to them with their given names. They did not die from the fire, they survived. She gives them power—they ran away from the fire. She then tells about a new crisis—their house burnt down—again they survived by running to someone else. Maia continues the narrative thread by telling: *They ran to Pippi Longstocking. Her house was not on fire. They ran to the house that couldn't burn and that was Maia's house. Her mother and father were at home. They ran from the rain.* Next, she does a change in authoring style, she begins to talk about *us*. This indicates a shift from fiction into a Buildung–narrative, *We had so strong arms, we were Pippi Longstocking. We could save them from the fire.* Maia introduces heroic identity markers into the story by doing this shift.

This co-narration can illustrate how two girls and I (as researcher), shape a narrative together and how this emerging process also embodies subtle, heteroglossic values and powerful identity potentials in the choice of protagonist, as well as in the turn by first putting themselves into the story and second by being *Pippi Longstocking*. The narrative can be read as an example that informs us about what these two girls explore, find important to talk about and to be. Rikke tells about the two of them, that they died from the fire, but survived.

The theme of survival that can be read from this narrative has also been described in other studies of children's play (Löfdahl, 2004; Paley, 1986) and narratives (Ødegaard, 2006). The words and powerful performances that are part of a *Pippi* aesthetic, have similarities to studies of children's meaning-making within the frame of multimodality and literacy (Dyson, 1997). Eva Maagerø (2004) describes a five-year-old boy's multimodal compositions, being an exploration over powerful men, a football keeper, the pirate Captain Sabretooth and a strong man. Authority is taken by the girls in the last three lines, *We had so strong arms. We were Pippi Longstocking. We could save them from the fire.* The costumes were chosen together with their families, they came dressed like *Pippi Longstocking* this particular day. The clothes were artefacts that made the playful talk and narrative identification easy. As such, the narrative about *Pippi* and the fire serves as a microcosmic site for conceptualising the intertextuality going on in co-narrative practice—a space where contradiction and negotiation are played out.

CONCLUSION

Children's narrative meaning-making is examined and exemplified as co-constructional process. Narrative meaning-making is seen as contextual, closely interwoven with the human, material, ideological and cultural context in which children take part. From a dialogical perspective, children's narratives as a co-construction can give knowledge of what children do with the resources that are made available for them and thereby how children bring in new meanings and become a participant of a wider cultural community.

REFERENCES

Bakhtin, M. M. (1981). *The dialogic imagination* (C. H. Emerson, Trans., M. Holquist, Ed., 2002 ed.). Austin, TX: University of Texas Press.
Bruner, J. S. (1990). *Acts of meaning* (2002 ed.). Cambridge, MA: Harvard University Press.
Dyson, A. H. (1997). *Writing superheroes: Contemporary childhood, popular culture, and classroom literacy* (1st ed.). New York, NY: Teachers College Press.
Hirschkop, K., & Shepherd, D. (2001). *Bakhtin and cultural theory* (2nd ed.). Manchester: Manchester University Press.
Junefelt, K. (2009). *The dialogic impact on early language development and thought.* Paper presented at The Second International Interdisciplinary Conference on Perspectives and Limits of Dialogism in Mikhail Bakhtin, Stockholm University, Sweden.
Lähteenmäki, M. (2004). Between relativism and absolutism: Towards an emergentist definition of meaning potential. In F. Bostad, C. Brandist, L. S. Evensen, & H. C. Faber (Eds.), *Bakhtinian perspectives on language and culture: Meaning in language, art and new media* (pp. 91–110). New York, NY: Palgrave MacMillan.
Löfdahl, A. (2004). *Förskolebarns gemensamma lekar: mening och innehåll.* Lund: Studentlitteratur.
Paley, V. G. (1986). *Boys and girls: Superheroes in the doll corner.* Chicago, IL: University of Chicago press.
Ødegaard, E. E. (2006). What's worth talking about? Meaning-making in toddler-initiated co-narratives in preschool. *Early Years—An International Journal of Research and Development, 26*(1), 79–92.
Ødegaard, E. E. (2007). *Meningsskaping i barnehagen: innhold og bruk av barns og voksnes samtalefortellinger.* Göteborg: Göteborgs universitet.
Ødegaard, E. E. (2011a). Narrative practice as a site for studying conditions for children's cultural formation. In P. K. Hansen (Ed.), *Working with stories: Narrative as a meeting place for theory, analysis and practice: European narratology network.* Denmark: University of Southern Denmark.
Ødegaard, E. E. (2011b). Narrative practices as a site for studying conditions for children's cultural formation. In P. K. Hansen (Ed.), *Working with stories: Narrative as a meeting place for theory, analysis and practice.* Kolding, Denmark: NarrNet, Syd Dansk Universitet
Ødegaard, E. E. (2011c). On the track of cultural formative practice:A chronotopic reading of young children's co-narrative meaning making. In J. White & M. Peters (Ed.), *Bakhtinian pedagogy: Opportunities and challenges for research, policy and practice in education across the globe.* New York, NY: Peter Laing.

Elin Eriksen Ødegaard
Center of Educational Research
Bergen University College

NARRATIVES ABOUT CHILDREN

This chapter will present and discuss research regarding the narratives that are shared between educators and families about children. The underlying perspective will be based on the interests of the child living in a world of change and transitions. Narratives about children are based on remembrance, observational data of past events or retelling of stories heard, but they shape futures when they are communicated, shared and acted upon. The control to empower and to disempower children on a personal and general level lies in the narrative (re)construction of reality. Narratives of children are to be found in education both in formative assessment (Carr & Lee, 2012) and in the area of narratives as part of pedagogical documentation (Rinaldi, 2009). This chapter will also present narratives about children told by teacher students and staff as stories from practice and narratives about children told by staff and families that occur in the cooperation between institutions and homes.

LEARNING STORIES? STUDENT AND STAFF STORIES ABOUT CHILDREN

In teacher education where developing pedagogical knowledge and situated judgment are forefronted, reflexivity is an essential aspect and therefore widely used. Several studies of and with staff and teachers students, were conducted from late 1990 up to today in Norway, inspired by narrative research on and with teachers (Goodson, 1992).

Stories about children were used as a tool for understanding children and pedagogical processes. Researching these stories as story types, it becomes clear that stories are told differently, in various forms that can be sorted in types of narratives. The identification of story types has demonstrated pedagogical focus, purpose and contains information about the teller and can therefore inform reflection on quality and ethics.

Louise Birkeland outlined five basic narrative types based on a close cooperation with kindergarten teachers on staff meetings all over Norway for many years (Birkeland, 1998, 2003, 2004; Ødegaard & Birkeland, 2002), a typology widely used in staff development and in teacher education and in researching the areas. In working with staff reflexivity, it became interesting to discuss with the teacher how the same events were told in different ways, from different perspectives, but also with a different basic tone difference. These varieties help us to discover how a story about children has a direction and a basic tone that will shape how we look upon a child, how we construct images on children and thereby shape their context. With reference to Jerome Bruner (Bruner, 1996; Bruner, Feldman, Hermansen,

& Molin, 2006) the concept of prism underlines how perspectives vary and that staff's stories about children are different from a story told by a child; how staff's perspectives will be of a different kind; and how types of story can shed light on staff's reflexivity and therefore sharpen sensitivity for children's perspectives, were motivation for staff training sessions. From a large collection of stories authored by staff and students, Birkeland (2004) suggested different types of stories about children:

- *Sunshine stories* are stories where the author makes the child the hero of the event. It is the new experience of the child that is picked up and dwelled on.
- *Success stories* are stories where the author lifts the author's own efforts to gain educational aims. The author's intention and efforts to achieve the aim are dwelled on.
- *Turning point stories* are stories where the author tells about a new and surprising event. The critical event is described in a way that turns the understanding of the child's capability or identity.
- *Vane stories* are stories where the author establishes a negative tone towards a child. The story could be a repetitive story about what a child does. Such stories can be a sign of low understanding and reflexivity of how children live contextual lives.
- *Blunder stories* are stories where the author reveals activities in a tone of self-criticism. Such stories could begin with lines like *I do not know if I dare to tell this...*

This typology has inspired other researcher to develop more types like humour stories, problem stories (Birkeland, 2004) and later solidarity stories[1]. Birkeland points to the fact that types of stories can differ also from the context the stories are told. Stories from the hallway could allow another type of story, the planned staff meeting. She found that the turning point stories and the blunder stories opened for reflexivity, while the sunshine stories and the success stories are more suited for pedagogical documentation. Vane stories are a type of stories that should alert a leader to investigate quality.

Stories from practice about children and their relations and activities can also be considered a genre. Bakhtin (1986) made a distinction between simple (primary) genres such as greetings and asking for something to drink and more complicated (secondary) genres which included written communication. Stories about children can be considered a complex genre.

With reference to a study of Norwegian students in teacher education, the aim was to get insight into personal and subjective aspects of processes working towards professionalism.

First year students are not beginners in life, even if they are in the beginning of a development towards teacher professionalism. Both students and teachers need to understand more of the complex problem areas they attend and where the children are situated. The aim of the study was to identify some characteristics of students' subjective processes in order to raise question for further development of teacher education. Research questions addressed were:

* How does narrative subjectivity appear in the students' stories of practice?
* What kind of stories do they tell?

In a dialogic analysis of 116 stories from first year students, events about children's activities were described. Aspects of time and where and when something happened, in which context, who said what to whom, with what kind of emotion and mood, and with what kind of ethical implications, were analytically described. Such analytic question allows for multiple meanings. A dialogic reading pursues a knowledge-philosophy that involves personal or subjective participation.

Students in this study write about their own experiences in a narrative genre. The stories reveal subjective experiences. The genre leads them to describe narrative subjectivity, whether they are conscious of it or not.

This study revealed that a *self* in some stories were completely absent, while the other student stories had a clear and actively participating self written into the stories. An utterance as 'I' here implies a social subjectivity, one's subjectivity related to other utterances (Ødegaard, 2015). In our context, this reveals that some of the students' stories describe children's activities and events in the institution without taking into consideration how a teacher will shape the condition for and be in relation to the children's activities and events. Qualitative analysis of dialogic narratives draws attention to the relationship between oneself and others (Sullivan, 2012).

Dialogic analysis enables the researcher to track insecurity and vulnerability because a student story teller assigns a role where the narrator has already predicted *other* [otherness]. This means that the narrator writes with the reader / readers in mind and that the story is already an answer in a wider social context. In a dialogical analysis expression of genres, discourses, kronotoper and emotional registers will be coded and described.

There is a distinction between studying subjectivity as simple or as complex. In a dialogical analysis, complex subjectivities are described. You place the conscious and sentient human being at the centre of analysis, but the consciousness and feelings are open, fluid and responding to others' words and actions. The language represents data that can be analysed as a sentient self, a self who is directed against others (for example, children), and who anticipates others' responses and replies (Bakhtin, 1986, calls this *adressivitet*). We will present some examples[2] of the different ways students establish their subjectivity with different types of narratives about children and about children and a student self.

A story of Success

LJ 2.2. years-old was sitting on the big bike. She uttered, *bus*. She stretched the legs towards the pedal, but did not reach it. She leaned further forward on the seat, but did still not succeed. She saw me standing and watching her from a distance a few meters away. She pointed behind her back down on the bike, looked at me with a pleading and helpless expression and whined. I understood that she wanted me to push her, but I replied to the silent question that the bike simply was too big. There was an overturned bike outside the cycle track beside her. I pointed to it and said that the bicycle over there was suitable for her. I walked over there, turned it up straight and put the bicycle on the road. LJ 2.2. came over to me and sat down on it, smiled and cycles off.

The student establishes himself as the hero of this story. The situation is described as an event where a child does not get what she tries to, namely cycling. The student understands the child's intent and supports the child in completing the project. The child is first described as sad (*whining*), later described as happy (*smiled*). The way the story is told establishes a subject who sees children, understands children, accommodates children's initiative and supports children to pursue their objectives. The student has positioned himself in relation to the child as one who can understand and act.

A Story of Sunshine

The children were all outside playing. It rains and it rains, there are ponds everywhere. Most of the children put wet sand in the sandpit. Girl 3 years old walked around alone where the other kids played and she looked worried and looked down. Some of the kids discovered her and called out for her and asked if she wanted to come along and make castles in the sandpit with them. She smiled and a big yes was uttered.

The story established a problem, a girl walking alone and sad. The story has a happy ending, the girl wanted to play with the other children and be happy. Here the narrator tells a story about a problem that was solved by inclusive children. This example is different than the first example. This is a story of practice about a child and a group of children without a narrative subject as a participating entity in history. The story mentions an incident that took place without the intervention of the student. The heroes of the story are *any of the other kids*. The heroes are created by the narrator. The narrator runs no risk by telling about children that include other children in the play, because it's the way we want it to be. We can see that the narrator draws attention to the children. The story is part of a discourse of *the competent child*. It is also a story that confirms what many 'know'. It may be a new recognition for the student to get a confirmation of what you have read in theory. Although the example does not have an articulated subject narrator, the story still communicates assumptions about the subject.

We can see a distinction between these two stories, of how they establish themselves in relation to the child in activity. In the story of success, it creates closeness between the narrator and the hero. In the second example, there is a distance between the narrator and the hero. There are still similarities between these two ways of portraying heroes. Stories of sunshine and success are stories with simple outcomes, who is the hero is obvious, and there is no kind of uncertainty incorporated in the stories.

Some of the other types of stories in the data articulated narrative subjectivity of an author 'I', but had a complexity that makes it worth studying further.

Some of the stories in the data material had a closeness between hero and author, a clear narrative subjectivity and an articulated uncertainty. Let us study an example:

A Blunder Story

The kindergarten often travels on excursions. This actual day we went to watch *Everything and Nothing* at the Children's Cultural Centre. When I arrived in kindergarten at 09:00 all the kids stood outside and were ready to go to town. [Here the story continues with detailed descriptions about the day.] When the kids were finished with lunch and the play we went back to the kindergarten. Some of the kids would go down the stairs themselves, while the others would take the elevator. I went with the three who would go down the stairs by themselves. When we were almost down, one child GJ 1.10 fell with her head hitting the doorsteps. Her forehead got swollen and I felt very sure it was my fault since I did not watch out for her. I know deep down that all children hit themselves, but anyway I think it was very uncomfortable since I was responsible for her there and then. But everything went fine, she cried a little, but soon everything was fine again. When we got back to the kindergarten about 13:30, I think a lot of the kids thought it was good to come back. Many of them were probably tired and exhausted after a long nice day.

In this narrative, the story is retold chronologically event for event. The story consists of six events. This example outlines the introduction, the first and the last section. It is the last event that is interesting to study in our context. The student describes an episode in which the student was alone with three small children. While going down the stairs one of the children fell, cried and got a big bump on the forehead. The narrator described his feelings. The student felt guilt—*It was my fault* and tried to reduce the feeling of guilt by comforting himself, *I know deep down that all children hurt themselves* and in the same sentence the student again describe the feeling of guilt, *but anyway I think it was uncomfortable since I was in charge there and then.* The student continues to comfort himself—*but everything went fine, she cried a little, but soon everything was fine again.* The student articulates an internal struggle between guilt and suppression of guilt. The subject-narrator becomes evident. In the other events the student described, he highlighted what 'we' do. When the child fell, 'I' enters in the description.

This episode shows an uncertainty associated with being responsible for children's safety. The story portrays the event so that it ends well. It is the student's secure and non-secure voice we can read here. The story holds a complex subjectivity because the hero of the story 'I' is unbalanced, unsure of what it means to take care of children's safety. It is a way of telling where the events told reveal uncertainty and where the narrator carries multiple perspectives in themselves, and where the narrator does not control the hero to the fullest (Sullivan, 2012).

With Birkeland typology, this story might be characterized as a story of blunder. A blunder story could have a greater potential for self-reflection than success or sunshine stories, because a blunder story honestly reveals mistakes, which could open the teller to change of thought and action (Birkeland, 2004). This student's story is, however. not a clear blunder story, because the student is working on a self-defence or diminishing the seriousness in the event.

These three stories about children reveal something about the teller, the student. Here we have seen ways that students establish narrative subjectivity in stories about children. We can see that both a clear participation and constitution of oneself as the hero in the story, as well an articulate uncertainty and ambivalence in these students' stories. Students also tell stories about children, where they constitute the children as the heroes.

FAMILIES AND STAFF'S STORIES ABOUT CHILDREN

For a teacher to understand and support a child in a complex and professional context, the teacher's knowledge goes beyond developmental knowledge. Children depend on their families and teachers and co-operation is supposed to make life an organic experience. Children, families and staff in early childhood settings are closely interrelated as human beings and this interrelatedness operates in a flux. This view implies that every event in a child's life will be conditioned by a range of more or less dynamic aspects. Children are simultaneously situated in time (duration and point of time) and space (place, distance, range and landscape) and have experiences with adults around them.

Stories about children will be a resource for teachers who work from within the child's socio-cultural situation (and location). In local kindergartens, nurseries and schools, the teachers meet children of social and genetic differences, a variety of languages and cultural heritages. With people travelling, ideas and culture travel with them across borders and media channels—a teacher will need to have both a global and a local awareness and knowledge in order to tell about children in ways of understanding and fairness. A *glocal* teacher might be better prepared to tune in to in local practices and grasp events where children take part.

A glocal teacher will consciously work to empower children, families and local communities. Several researchers have described the mistake of using universal pedagogical methods in multicultural and multi-ethnic classrooms, and some also offer culture-sensitive and appropriate approaches (Balto, 2009; Gupta, 2006; Mannion, 2010; Paley, 1997; Tobin, 2013). Narratives about children bear the promise and possibility to do so.

Children's play worlds can entail data for studying children's identity and sense of belonging. As shown by Margaret Carr and Wendy Lee, narrative can be well suited for teachers as researchers (Carr & Lee, 2012). They show how children are connected to a wider community outside the early childhood institution with the use of learning stories and descriptive photos. Teachers' stories about children, evidenced by the children and their families, are used as formative assessment in early childhood institutions in New Zealand, an approach developed through research.

In a cooperative study about children's stories as a means to strengthen the relationship between staff and parents, stories about children had a double purpose. On the one hand, the staff were writing stories about children to better remember children's activities during the day, so that parents could get a story in the hallway in the afternoon. The staff also wrote stories for each child in their portfolio. The researcher recieved a copy, so that data were produced in order to find what themes staff communicated about children (Ødegaard, 1998).

CONCLUDING REMARKS—STRENGTHENING PEDAGOGY FROM NARRATIVES ABOUT CHILDREN

We have outlined narratives about children as fundamentally relational. Aristotle takes up two ways to react to *poiesis* (make) and *praxis* (action) which in turn requires two different forms of judgment (Aristotle, 1973). Such practical wisdom reflects the personal qualities and abilities that can be called virtue, as the ability to make wise pedagogical judgements. Aristotle thought wisdom came with experience, which is a key aspect when working with enhancing quality in early childhood institutions. Practice is thus an arena for working with the practical wisdom—judgment. Biesta points out the distinction between an socialization and subjectification (Biesta, 2013). We understand this as a distinction between two different ideals of practice, namely an ideal in which the adult actors (staff, parents and students) are expected to act as models or supervisors for children (socialization). Another ideal is the expectation that the adults will act as the adults believe it is right to act. There is not necessarily any contradiction between these dimensions, but there might be, because pedagogical situations are never identical, and because the relationship between an adult actor and children never will be equal.

As we have seen above, narratives about children can reveal narrative subjectivity in the author of the story—a student, a teacher or a family member. Gert Biesta writes about the 'beautiful risk' in education. Education will always be 'risky' because education is a meeting between people (Biesta, 2013). Students should not be regarded as objects to be formed and disciplined, but as empowered and responsible entities. Such a view of education requires that you become involved in pedagogical events beyond yourself, but also include yourself in relation to children.

Seeing education as a fundamental dialogic process opens up for stories about children related to the other as another child, a parent, a teacher and so on. To write and tell about children gives staff and families a good opportunity to meet children with prudence. Students, staff and families on their part, have the opportunity to develop their narrative subjectivity and to express what they read and understand about children and themselves as responsible and professional subjects.

NOTES

[1] Learning stories is an obvious type of stories about children that is developed in New Zealand (Carr, 2001; Carr & Lee, 2012) and spread elsewhere.
[2] The examples are also presented in (Ødegaard; 2015).

REFERENCES

Aristoteles. (1973). *Etikken*. Oslo: Gyldendal.

Biesta, G. (2013). *The beautiful risk of education*. Boulder, CO: Paradigm Publication.

Birkeland, L. (1998). *Pedagogiske erobringer: om praksisfortellinger og vurdering i barnehagen*. Oslo: Pedagogisk forum.

Birkeland, L. (2003). Storytelling and staff training: A narrative approach to reflective practice. In U. O. Greenwich (Ed.), *Occasional papers* (pp. 115–122). London: University of Greenwich.

Birkeland, L. (2004). Fortellinger der færnger og fanger—Praksisfortellinger og personaleudvikling i børnehaven. In S. I. Mørch (Ed.), *Pædagogiske praksisfortellinger* (pp. 110–125). Viborg: Systime Academic.

Bruner, J. S. (1996). *The culture of education*. Cambridge, MA: Harvard University Press.

Bruner, J. S., Feldman, C. F., Hermansen, M., & Molin, J. (2006). *Narrative, learning and culture*. Copenhagen: New Social Science Monographs.

Carr, M. (2001). *Assessment in early childhood settings: Learning stories*. Thousand Oaks, CA: P. Chapman Publication.

Carr, M., & Lee, W. (2012). *Learning stories: Constructing learner identities in early education*. Los Angeles, CA: Sage.

Goodson, I. (1992). *Studying teachers' lives*. London: Routledge.

Rinaldi, C. (2009). *I dialog med Reggio Emilia*. Bergen: Fagbokforlaget.

Ødegaard, E. E. (2015, March). Kompleks subjektivitet—sikre og usikre fortellinger fra praksis. In E. E. Ødegaard & M. S. Økland (Eds.), *Fortelinger fra praksis—profesjonalitet, identitet og barnehagelærerutdanning*. Bergen: Fagbokforlaget.

Ødegaard, E. E. (1998). Fortell om meg da jeg var liten Fortellingen som mulighet i samarbeidet mellom barnehage og hjem. *Norsk Pedagogisk Tidsskrift, 6*, 375–385.

Ødegaard, E. E., & Birkeland, L. (2002). *Tusen erfaringer søker fortellinger: gleder og utfordringer med fortellinger i barnehagens pedagogiske arbeid: rapport fra et FOU-prosjekt*. Bergen: Høgskolen i Bergen.

Elin Eriksen Ødegaard
Center of Educational Research
Bergen University College

NARRATIVES BY CHILDREN

Narratives are rule-governed, and can be used to understand the rational and social aspect of experiences. But they are also meandering, non-linear, cryptic and idiosyncratic, filled with layers of material, as are the minds that create them. The wilderness is worth exploring. (Engel, 2000, para 41)

INTRODUCTION

Stories and story-telling practices have a long history and are closely connected to language, human social formations and the historically emerging vision of individuality and the modern person (Bamberg, 2012; Cohen, et al., 2011; Kuntay & Ervin-Tripp, 1997; Liles, 1987). We have connected with this history in Chapters 1 and 3. Sharing lived experiences is a way of expressing one's self and to process or be self-reflective. As Clandinin and Connelly (1995) share the telling, retelling and reliving assist in the exploration of meaning and meaning making of our lives, experiences and thoughts. Sharing also allows for others to consider, reconsider and ponder. Like adult narratives, children's narratives "are almost always autobiographical at one level or another, and (like adult narratives) they can be treated as both literature and psychological phenomena" (Engel, 2000, para 2). From a psychologists perspective, narratives are viewed as the vehicle through which children become socialised (Engel, 2000) especially as there has been a gradual shift in focus on thinking of children's narratives as a solitary and private activity to one that is visible and understandable (Nelson, 1985; Engel, 1995; Brice-Heath, 1985). This way of thinking about children's narratives aligns with developmental psychologists and how narrative is believed to be a construct of a knowable, rational, and socialized child (Nelson 1998). This approach reiterates that communication, learning and "care of children that fully meets their needs will automatically have benefits for all the persons involved, and for society at large" (Trevarthen et al., 2003 p. 6). And highlights how significant contribution to education and how narratives by children are powerful contributions to understanding perspectives, valuing voice and inclusive practice.

This chapter explores narratives told by children. Narrative devices that children use in their own story telling to create meaning are introduced as too the varying structures that are used in order to share those stories. Two case studies are shared, firstly a case study is shared from the Australian context that looks at how five- to seven-year-old children engaged with visual narratives to tell their lived experiences of learning and teaching. The second case, also from Australia, presents visual narratives from at four and seven-year-old children who are sharing their thoughts about what is important to them. Both cases share the paring of digital still photographs with verbal or written narratives to offer examples of how image-based research can be a powerful methodology to explore meaning making and place the young person at the heart of both narratives haring and exploration of lived experience—in this case of learning and teaching moments in the early childhood classroom.

NARRATIVES BY CHILDREN—DEVICES IN STORY TELLING

Children develop language skills from birth as they participate in interactions with others who have more mature language (Stadler and Ward, 2005). Engel (2000, para 40) reminds us in considering narrative by children that:

> Much of the time children tell stories in which they shift back and forth between transparency and opacity. They tell something, and then become covert. Stories are on the one hand a means of revealing information to others; on the other hand they offer rich opportunities for dissembling, fabricating, and hiding material.

When thinking about narratives by children it is important to consider the context of developing the emotional milestones that is connected to story telling, especially in relation to changing relationships and the sharing of experience through intentional communication (Sethi et al., 2000; Vondra et al., 2001). Alongside emotional thinking develops with narrative imagination and language. This development conditions the expression of self-esteem in a personal identity (self-image as learner, communicator and contributor to all being seen as learners) (Lewis, 1993; Marshall, 1997; Target and Fonagy, 1996). Bruner has argued that narratives serve as a cooling vessel for children, allowing them to gain first symbolic, and then emotional and cognitive, distance over the experiences they recount. When feeling (rivalry, love, anger, frustration, care, etc.) takes shape in a story, the words and narrative form both embody and contain the feelings, and thus give the narrator distance from her/ his own affect.

Children often use narratives to create a boundary between "wild and private" (Engel, 2000, para 3). Freeman (2010) and Sarbin (2004) highlight imagination in relationship to narrative inquiry. Narrative construction can mean see imaginings as embodied and perceptual knowing whereby "we draw on our rememberings and enable our *as if* stories" (Huber et al., 2013). Imagining is connected to becoming.

A child's memory and imagination grow in the first three years, and thus assisting in extending the world that can be shared and explored with others (Emde et al., 1997; Fivush & Hudson, 1982; Nelson, 1982; Rovee-Collier & Gerhardstein, 1997; Trevarthen, 2001). Adults respond by increasing their support, guidance and instruction. As young children at age of around one year interact with adults the 'scaffolding' of the experience that the child is building occurs to support and assist in the reinforcing of the learning and memory for the child (Erickson, 1996; Rogoff, 1990, 1998; Vygotsky, 1978). As a child progresses to being two and three years of age an adult scaffolds and models the language, learning and cognitive development (Bruner, 1983; Masur, 1997).

Beginning from the ages of three or four years, children begin using story telling (Stadler & Ward, 2005). They are a useful tool for the development of oral language (Morrow, 1985; Stadler and Ward, 2005), and have links to bridging literacy development (Hedberg and Westby, 1993). Stadler and Ward (2005) have reported that there is much support for "using narratives as an effective format for the facilitation of oral language skills because stories require more complex language than that needed for daily conversations" (p. 71). Narratives assist children "in moving from sharing function of conversations to teaching function of written language by imparting lessons based on one's experiences" (Stadler & Ward, 2005, p. 73). Narratives thus provide opportunities for children to develop a higher level of language, associated to explicit vocabulary required when being a story teller, before they become readers. The use of pronouns and temporal connections such as when, so and while have been associated to this higher language use while being a story teller (Stadler & Ward, 2005).

It has been noted by Applebee (1978), as too Vygotsky (1978) that narratives are related to children's development. Narratives facilitate the use of language to monitor, reflect and communicate loved experiences. In order to communicate a story "children must have knowledge of the following concepts: temporal and cause-effect relationship and theory of the minds (knowing that others can think and feel differently than we do)" (Stadler & Ward, 2005, p. 73). Applebee (1978) presented six developmental level of narrative appropriate for two- to six-year-old children, based on European story telling traditions, that build on elements of centering (focus on a topic) and chaining (sequencing events). These include:

- Heaps (unrelated statements that label or describe),
- Sequence (statements based on a central topic),
- Primitive narratives (statements based on a central topic with perceptual and temporal links),
- Unfocused chain (temporally related statements without central topic),
- Focused chain (temporally related statements based around a central topic), and
- True narrative (story telling with developed plot and statements that are temporal and related to a central topic with a theme or moral).

Stadler and Ward (2005) in their work with three- to five-year-old pre-school children explored a variety of narratives, and further extended Applebee's (1978) work by analysing narratives as:

- Labelling (previously heaps),
- Listing (previously sequence),

- Connecting (previously primitive narratives),
- Sequencing (previously focused chain), and
- Narrating (previously true narrative).

The work that Stadler and Ward (2005) have undertaken understand that narrative development is important for all children and when teachers know how narratives develop, what level stories their students tell, and how to foster story telling at higher levels, they are better equipped to help all children develop oral narrative skills critical for ordering personal experiences, communication, concept formation, and literacy preparation (p. 79). These are important life skills associated to communication and voice.

Labov (1972) summarized narratives as an abstract anticipating a topic, orientation, complicating action, resolution, evaluation and coda. He considered young children's narratives to be likely to be retold and would develop these stable structures. The work of Kuntay and Ervin-Tripp (1997) builds on the research of Labov (1972) especially in relation to conversational narratives and those that are most likely to be scaffolded mainly by adult probing. Kuntay and Ervin-Tripp (1997, p. 115) found that most children observed in preschools "did not produce stories for other children who gave them no prompts". Rather "it was adults who often supported children's elicited stories with prompts to get started and to continue, thus altering the narrative order and scaffolding the normative features". These are especially important findings when looking at young people's conversations narratives in educational settings. Adult, or educator, scaffolding can significantly impact children's narratives, and with careful guidance can assist greatly in establishing more detailed narratives to support learning and teaching. Of note is also that in educational settings such as preschools, Kuntay and Ervin-Tripp (1997) found that "stories implicitly invited related stories from other participants [young children]" (p. 116) often with spontaneity within natural conversational settings or environments when connections can be made to the same topic. In building from this it was found that young children's narratives seem to be organised around turn taking, that is that although the genre of narratives is often identified with a continuous speech by one single speaker, the conversational narrative when developed by an adult who is probing can illicit structure in narratives such as this (Kuntay & Ervin-Tripp, 1997, p. 119):

- *Retelling* (stories that are retold already have a basis in form, and a reteller has the knowledge of how the first occasion was evaluated by the audience. Retelling is likely to conform to culturally reinforced structure),
- *Prompting* (stories that are told in response to narrow questions or to make particular conversational points are more likely to select a time in the narrative to begin which does not entail a build-up or elaboration. But prompts, collaboration, and evaluations from an audience indicate attentiveness and willingness to hear a long story, leading the speaker to turn what could have starts as a tactical move into a performance),

- *Cues from prior stories* (Children's attempts to top the previous story by incorporating different facets of their similar experiences lead to a pattern of overlapping these, allowing continuity and elaboration of latent topic, emulations of form, and ellipsis due to presupposition), and
- *Supporting other speech events/acts* (narratives that are volunteered to serve function such as exemplification, justification, explanation, and specifying source of information get structurally organized displaying features marking their pragmatic significance. The telling may include just the high point, or just constructed speech, or just a description).

The child telling a story can actively negotiate the distinctions between what is revealed and what is concealed, between following the conventions of one's culture and breaking those conventions. Children use stories (their own and other people's) to differentiate between what they consider to be the domain of fact and the domain of fiction. Narratives allow children to construct domains, and at the same time to create permeable boundaries around those domains (Engel, 2000, para 3).

Just as verbal communication is developed so too is the communication of narratives visually. Young children use story telling as a way of constructing spheres of reality (Engel, 2000). As Engel (2000) remind us:

> After more than a decade of rich, expansive, and precise work on children's narratives, to close the gap between the clinician's focus on content and the researcher's focus on form. It is apparent that the form of children's stories reveals much about what concerns them, and that content can reveal much about how they organize the world mentally. The action of telling a story is one way children negotiate the boundaries between inner and outer life. Children express and consider their ideas, experiences, and impulses by embodying them in stories. The process, form, and content of stories allow them to discover the boundaries between what is revealed and what is concealed, and to develop some control over those boundaries. (para 39)

Engel (2000) reminds us when adult authors use narratives to create boundaries they choose rhetorical techniques deliberately. For example an author may use autobiography as a screen or curtain that confuses the reader further about what is fact and what is fiction. A child's use demonstrates an important developmental difference, in that it may use narrative devices and the narrative form itself to create these spheres of reality for oneself. The symbolic action the child creates spheres that one can reflect on. The child can explore the boundaries of those spheres, and vary what one reveals and conceals. As an adult the boundaries set are due so guided by audience. The young child, on the other hand, does so for oneself as much as she does so for a listener.

By about three years young children are drawing a variety of familiar things, and making drawings to illustrate stories or narratives (Light and Barnes, 1995). The ways that a child is learning to communicate ideas and imagination creatively is revealed and shares more about the growth of thinking (Tizard and Hughes, 1984).

RICHNESS OF CHILDREN'S VISUAL NARRATIVES

There is a tendency in education to think of children's narratives or creative narrative or visual narrative purely as a verbal element or verbal communication, either spoken or written (Wright, 2011). However focus on the "visual narrative related to children's drawings, [images or photographs] emphasizes and offers the richness of the accompanying interactions as children tell and act out the underlying stories" (p. 8). Young people can visualize as well as articulate, as well as depict. Children can represent "people, places, objects and events...told through graphic action – mark making that depicts ideas and feelings on paper in real time" (p. 158). The young person's combination of visual and verbal content interactively present a message through both "denotation and connotation," with such "crossing over of modes is what makes visual narrative such a powerful medium for children's communication of ideas and expression of feelings" (p. 161). Structurally a visual narrative is spontaneous. It unfolds over time and moves between loose themes, in whatever order or sequence they evolve for the child communicating their experiences. The "content and structure of young children's narratives are often different in important ways from that which typically engages adults" (Wright, 2011, p. 162). This looseness is often referred to as configurational signs, that signs that are ever changing (Eagan, 1988). As a new concept develops a child may go back, re-engage with and revisit a photograph, image or visual to further add to and explain their experiences, feelings, ideas and connections.

Children draw and create meaning instinctively from an early age (Wright, 2011). They do so in a way that allows them to explore in process and concepts to discover meaning. "Drawing and other art media provide young children with opportunities to share their inner worlds, often more effectively than if communicating through other forms" (Wright, 2011, p. 157). Through graphic telling or visual narratives, children conceive the world, rather than merely render it, and is motivated through authentic learning (Wright, 2011; Thompson, 2002), creating a way for new learning to be connected to old. Work visually provides an entry point and a "structuring form for children to have a voice and for others to hear that voice" (Wright, 2011).

Giving a voice to young children through art should one of the core businesses of early children's education. Proving opportunities to compose through visual narratives completes children's rights to play and discover the world around them (Thompson, 2002; Wright, 2011) and to discover ways to understand, explore and know about the world and others. One cannot overlook the power and insightful sharing a young child can share when producing a visual narrative. The dialogue (written or verbal) that accompanies the visual supports and provides an opportunity for symbolization or as Vygotsky (1978) calls, providing a graphic speech (Dyson, 1982). Visual narratives support the communication of thinking. This method of thinking, sharing and assigning meaning, supports the co-construction of one way of understanding the world (Bruner, 1980; Lemon, 2008), providing "images, messages, and insights into their worlds to help us see through the eyes of the creator" (Wright, 2011, p. 162).

WHAT MIGHT NARRATIVES BY CHILDREN LOOK LIKE?

In the next section of the chapter two cases are presented where young children have been invited to be digital image makers to share their voice. In this way of working narratives by children are produced. Two different methods are shared that see young children between the age of five to seven years generate their own digital still photographs used a portable and hand held digital camera. In the first case the young people captured their learning for a school year. The teacher was a co-researcher with the young people. In the second case a one off observation was made in a learning environment by the researcher. Handing one digital camera to the young children offered opportunity for the researcher to invite the young people to share their voice about school, rather than an interpretation from an outsider to the learning environment. One student inadvertently became the research assistant, taking on board the role of introducing all his peers to the researcher and making sure that all had the opportunity to use the camera, download the images, and talk immediately to why the image was important to them.

A Case of Young Children Capturing Their Learning in the Learning Environment

In this case we are provided insights into five- to seven-year-old children telling their stories through visual narratives. In seeing children are capable digital linage makers, a case study is shared that highlights how young children can share their lived experiences of being learners in the classroom environment through the generation of visual narratives. This teacher inquiry provided one perspective of how visual methods was implemented in one Australian school setting to engage young children with their learning and reflection as part of the early childhood curriculum. My voice as author of this chapter is shared as this research was undertaken in the learning classroom where I was teacher. The use of visual methods has opened up new ways of perceiving the early childhood classroom. The use of 'image as a key data source' (Moss, 2008b, p. 25) especially generated by young participants (Lemon, 2008) is a relatively new innovation within education. In this research it has become evident that text and images work alongside each other as a way for interrogating taken for granted polices and deeper meaning of lived experiences of classroom life (Richardson, 1990; 2000). As MacNaughton (2005) reiterates:

> Classrooms are replete with texts and their meanings...[and] fill classroom life. Different forms of text enter classroom life in different ways but as they enter it they each contribute to the equity meanings that are produced, lived and experiences by children and adults in the early childhood classroom. (p. 76)

The early childhood children of this study were young image-makers telling and showing their stories of teaching and learning through the generation of their own still digital photographs and subsequent reflection, forming visual narratives. Each child contributed to the sharing of their lived experiences of the early childhood classroom and contributed to the formation of a learning community. Most importantly each child's voice was valued and respected for the contribution, insights, perspective it provided. Visual narratives were generated through the integration of one digital camera (see Lemon 2008 for details on method), which was used within the classroom by each child. In this way young children were invited to enact responsibility in using technology in the classroom. Trust was important for this aspect and when empowered with possibilities of using technology meaningfully, the early childhood children were very capable digital photographers who engaged with the opportunity to explore technology. The children openly shared their voice and insights to the teacher and peers about the technology and of teaching and learning accompanied with development in confidence to explore visual learning. Exploring and integrating the portable hand-held technology of the digital camera promoted openness to perspective from the children and to work with peers that they hadn't had an opportunity to work with before, with many engaging in peer teaching and role reversal of what/who is a traditional teacher and learner in the classroom. This was particularly significant as the emphasis on a democrat classroom affirmed a sense of belonging for all students as well in addition to the formation of a learning community.

Verbal responses to a photographic visual became a regular occurrence in the classroom. The children built on the process of using a digital camera in the classroom and reflected on their own photographs one-to-one with their teacher, or in whole class or small peer group contexts. The children were encouraged to offer their photographs for learning experiences that promoted reflection through mediums such as wall displays, graffiti walls, or graphic organizers. The growth in the children's reflective skills were indicated when they drew incomplete sections of a photograph and provided more in depth information to support the narratives. Often in small group or whole class activities a photograph was used for reflection with sentence starters being used as both prompts and as a modelling strategy. Reflection was undertaken in written, verbal, or visual modes, providing students with an opportunity to use their preferred mode of reflection.

Over time the children gained confidence in using language to explore and describe what they had experienced. A very positive aspect of this study was the development of students' language skills, both verbal and written, through the reflective process. Growth was particularly noticeable in students with low self-esteem and among those experiencing learning difficulties associated with reading and writing. Through taking their own photographs and then reflecting via their preferred modes, students' linguistic skills improved, in particular their syntactical structures. Self-esteem and personal identity also significantly changed as the children learnt they could share and would be valued for their voice (Lewis, 1993).

90

The children's visual narratives revealed the day-to-day experiences of the early childhood classroom. I noted in my journal:

My teaching is about facilitating teaching and learning, where it is student centred and I guide students through experiences related to the development of the curriculum content. The visual narratives emerging, those with and those without text, show mixed practices of teacher/student centred learning. I questioned, is it me and my pedagogical practices, or is it the influence of past teachers (prep and kindergarten), specialist teachers or other stakeholders where some learning experiences and reactions had the children waiting for a more teacher-centred directions. Is school about control or exploration? Reflection (Term 3, Week 3 – Tuesday)

Connecting with my reflection, Goodman (1978) and Schön (1987) claim we continually make and remake versions of the world using words, numerals, pictures, sounds, and other symbols, a world that is constructed through versions, as opposed to a world that is found or ready-made. The lived experiences that the children of this study shared through their visual narratives showed a mix of indoctrinated rules and regulations versus experiences of freedom to inquire (hooks, 1994). By indoctrinated rules and regulations I refer, for example, to children sitting in silence on the floor, lining up in a silent straight line outside the classroom door before entering the classroom, completing worksheets and only talking when asked to talk.

Why do the children line up outside the classroom door? Why is it that I feel like colleagues think I don't seem in control if the children are not in a line? Is it a matter of control or is it a matter of respecting the conversations that occur when we all congregate outside the classroom door in a huddle. The celebrations, new discoveries and problem solving are much more exciting than silence and no inquiry. Reflection (Term 3, Week 3 – Friday)

In the learning environment of this study children were encouraged to engage in conversations with each other and with classroom visitors to think and explore meaning making and to construct knowledge. In our learning community, I encouraged a sense of belonging, meaning making and a valuing of authentic experiences. Moreover, the children were encouraged to believe that everyone in the classroom is a learner – student, teacher, and visitors – and that we can all learn from each other. Through the children's photographs I was able to reflect on changes I had undertaken to develop an inquiry based, student-centred classroom. A question that I had initially posed when working with these children was *Why does the teacher have to be the only person in the classroom who can give the acknowledged* tick of approval *for work?* Over time and with scaffolding of the process of creating visual narratives the children began to explore alternative ways of acknowledging and celebrating success—both their own and their peers' work. Conversations regularly occurred amongst the children with comments that encouraged their peers such as, *Look at Max's writing. How good does it look?* (Hannah), and James saying to Olive,

I really like how you designed your robot. Can you show me how you did it? The process of the children's visual narratives provided opportunities for a supportive, celebratory discourse to be enacted.

Student sharing and engaging with each other's work contributed to the sense of being a community of learners and diminished the reliance upon teacher-centred practices. Sharing went beyond an activity that occurred in the morning classroom schedule into one where the children shared knowledge and explored questions with peers. Hannah, Ben, Rose and Gemma's photos (Figure 6 to Figure 9) show this happening as they reinforce knowledge, ask questions, think about learning links, and reflect on their learning environment. In the session when these photographs were taken, roles were reversed with the child leading the inquiry sitting in the 'teacher's chair' while I sat on the floor with the other children. Generally the teacher is seated at a level above the children and while interactions can and do occur between the learner and teacher, the focus is primarily on the teacher (see Figure 4 and Figure 5). By placing myself on the floor, I was not the focal point, and this challenged the children's preconceived notions of the classroom thus transforming the traditional participation and identity constructions in a community of practice (Wenger, 1998).

Figure 4. Miss Lemon (Gemma).

Miss Lemon is sitting on the floor with us. I don't think I have seen this before... hmmmm... no, but she always does it (Gemma).

She is a great teacher. She listens and shows us her ideas. (Gemma's photo of Olive teaching the class).

Figure 6 is Rose's photo of Jane teaching the class about her home country, America, through a traditional doll she brought to school from home.

Figure 5. Olive (Gemma).

Figure 6. Jane teaching (Rose).

Figure 7 shows Ben's photo of Gemma recording student comments on the whiteboard during a brainstorming session.

Figure 8 is Hannah's photo of an experiment connected to an integrated inquiry about recycling, reducing and reusing.

Hannah's photo of predictions for an experiment to be carried out about food degrading over time is shown at Figure 9.

93

Figure 7. Gemma (Ben).

Figure 8. Recycling, reducing and reusing (Hannah).

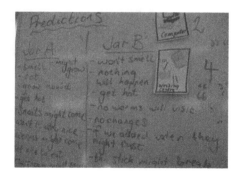

Figure 9. Predictions (Hannah).

Figure 10. James and his brother.

Figure 11. James teaches the class with his brother.

Figure 10 and Figure 11 and the accompanying dialogue are demonstrations of the interaction and inquiry during a session where James was teaching the class, about coral he had seen while on an interstate trip to the coast with his family.

James[1]   *Would you like to get a piece of paper? [talking to the class who are sitting on the floor looking up at James]. Miss Lemon can you take photos so we can look back at what I'm teaching?*

[Class moves to collect pencil cases, a book to lean on and paper. James is speaking to his brother who he has invited from the prep class. He has joined us to watch his brother, James, share their interstate trip. They speak in German [mother tongue] to each other, clarifying the steps about what James is going to teach the class].

James   *Follow the way my brother draws it [in English].*

[James has invited his brother now to join him in teaching the class].

James   *First do a T... like this...just like this and curve it around.and you don't have to do it very good.and then you put that on this side and nearly to the bottom...it's like a love heart on one side...then put a line. [Pause].*

> *And another one [pause and watching the class] then inside you put this [draws a line] and then if you would like to you can put this one [draws another line on the angle contributing to the picture of coral].*

Cameron   *What is it? [looking up from his page and at James creating his masterpiece on the whiteboard].*

James   *It is coral [inspired from his recent family holiday to Queensland, state of Australia]. Then put this on the side [continues adding lines to his drawing to expand the coral effect].*

Olive   *This is really cool.*

Claire   *I didn't know how to draw this before.*

Cameron   *Yeah, coral is cool.*

James   *Here are mini shapes in the coral. It can be a little hard to draw because I am showing you exact. It's getting harder and harder.*

Gemma   *It is complicated. But we can do it. We are risk takers.*

James   *Then you add this part and then you draw these lines. It is actually sideways so you have to actually put it around this way if you want to [motioning to classmates to turn the paper around to the vertical]. You do a wobble [wobbly line]……and so on [continues to draw without talking, the class follows, watching every move].*

In the above excerpt, James called on his brother to assist him with his knowledge sharing. As part of the community, parents, siblings or other teachers would often join the class taking on varying roles, such as listening to reading, visiting experts or as learners themselves. The following photographs show the children's observations of some of these occurrences:

Figure 12 shows Charles' photograph of a peer's parent helping children in the classroom read.

Figure 13 is Olive's photograph of a parent visitor. She had heard from her daughter about parents visiting the classroom and wanted to experience being a part of the community.

Figure 12. Parent helping (Charles).

Figure 13. Parent visitor (Olive).

Figure 14. A teacher from another grade (Cameron).

Cameron photographs a teacher from another grade working with his peers on a literacy activity focusing on use of letters to construct words (see Figure 14).

The German language teacher who visited the classroom twice a week for specialist lessons with the children became engaged in the production of visual narratives. She regularly conversed with the children about their reflections and was also curious about the practices she observed. Following our discussions, we decided to invite children to take digital photos and to then view them immediately on the laptop screen and reflect as a class. The following images show this process of a visiting teacher becoming a part of the learning community, learning from the children, and integrating visual narratives into her practice as a strategy for reflection on teaching and learning.

Meaningful resources were photographed (Figure 15 to Figure 17) by the children and these images highlighted the importance and value they placed on them in their learning experiences. As Wenger implies, meaningful resources "enhance their [children's] participation, opening their horizons so that they can put themselves on learning trajectories they can identify with, [while] involving them in actions, discussions, and reflections that make a difference to the communities they value" (Wenger, 1998, p. 10).

Figure 15. German language teacher.

Figure 16. German language teacher.

Figure 17. German language teacher.

A CASE OF TELL ME WHAT IS IMPORTANT TO YOU

Tales of an early childhood classroom are shared in this visual narrative. It is constructed of the digital photographs and words of young children aged between four and seven years. They are members of a class from a school located in Melbourne, Victoria. Each child participated in a two-year prep program aimed at preparing them for school readiness. Focus is on play based learning with opportunities to develop academic, emotional and social skills. As researcher I was invited to participate in the research however, as shared in Chapter 9, the approach was very much about research on children. Part of my role was to observe the children in their learning setting and to provide a report about their learning patterns. On my second visit to the classroom I decided to change my approach and sought permission to research with the children, to gather their voice about their experiences of school. I shared with the teachers and parents how inviting the children to be digital image makers would empower them to share their narratives while building skills in use of mobile digital technology, social skills in taking turns as well as listening and communicating capabilities. This case thus builds on learning the work of image based methods, learning stories (Carr, 2001), and observation methods.

The students worked with me for one and a half hours while they concurrently participated in the learning activities facilitated by the teacher. Each student one by one was invited to work with me. Initially I thought I would approach the children, develop a relationship and then invite them to use the digital camera. However, the camera captivated one student called Gabriele. He was adamant that every one of his classmates could take turns at using the technology. The trust and mutual respect of a visitor (me) to the classroom shown to the students was quickly and intuitively accepted. Gabriele was determined that he could assist me in making sure everyone had a turn. So he took on the role of research assistant. He wrote down all his classmates names on my not book so I could make sure all were included, noting at the same time that her could practice his writing. He then approached peers one at a time to come and sit with me, have a lesson on using the digital camera, roam freely around the classroom capturing what was important to them, and then returning for assistance to download the images onto a laptop for immediate viewing and sharing of the story they wished to share. This narrative was captured by my typing on the laptop as we had a conversation. There was no prodding for extra information, rather this was led by the young people as to how many images they wished to generate and how much they wanted to share.

The three sets of visual narratives presented are tales of an early childhood classroom, one moment in time. Text is the voice of a young person. Juxtaposed is the intertextuality of the children's digital images. They are presented as per the young person's direction, and only those they wish to present in this tale are displayed in the tale. It should be noted that parental permission has been granted for this way of working and for sharing in publications such as this book.

THE VISUAL NARRATIVES BY ASHAM, FIVE YEARS OF AGE.

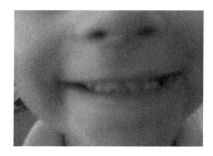

Figure 18. Luka (Asham).

A picture of Luka. He plays with me. I can see his teeth. He is my friend.

Figure 19. Packing up (Asham).

Packing up. It was snack time. We have to pack up so we have room for snack. Everyone helps to pack up...before and after. (Figure 19.)

Figure 20. Luka is my friend (Asham).

Luka. He has a bandage he went to hospital because he fell down the rocks. My sister broke her arm...because she was running ...all around it...and lots of blood. had to go to hospital to get bandaged.

I like about to school play with the castle and taking a shower and playing outside at recess. I went outside and get a photo.

THE VISUAL NARRATIVES BY GURJOT, SIX YEARS OF AGE

I like playing. I play outside and in here [classroom]. I like to make things and play outside.

Figure 21. Kicking balls (Gurjot).

The class is kicking the balls. I had a go at kicking. It was good. I like the step kicking part. I can kick to the big blue mat and then it bounced and came back to me. Nothing is hard at school. My most favourite thing is playing.

THE VISUAL NARRATIVES BY CHANTELLE, SIX YEARS OF AGE

Figure 22. Siena (Chantelle).

Siena... a picture with her wonderful picture. Siena is my friend.

101

Figure 23. Siena holding up her work (Chantelle).

Siena with her two papers that she made.

Figure 24. Heva (Chantelle).

I took a picture of Heva cause she is my friend. She starts with a "H". I like Heva because she always plays with me and she's always nice.

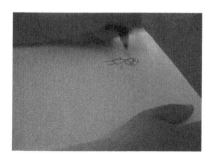

Figure 25. Heva's drawing (Chantelle).

That's Heva's drawing. She is very good. She draws a person and I like it.

Figure 26. Mea (Chantelle).

That's Mea. I took a picture of Mea because she plays with me at after school care. I go there today.

CONCLUSION

Narratives by children share the inquiry into their lived experiences by carefully providing opportunity to explore the facilitation of oral language skills and the complexity of daily conversations. The visual narrative shared shows how children can communicate their lived experiences in the learning environment. They are capable photographers of their world. As Stadler and Ward (2005) have researched, the narratives provide opportunity for the children to learn from their own experiences and from others around them. When narrative is valued and a regular part of learning opportunities, reflection, making connections, and feeling valued become central elements. Alongside is the development of language, pronouns and key story telling devices.

Children's narratives provide opportunity to hear their voice. In honouring their perspective and valuing their contribution it is possible to see young children as capable communicators of their lived experiences. The case study shared from an Australian context reminds us how this is possible through one example that engage both the generation of digital still photographs and the sharing of narrative verbally or in written form. This research contributes to the field of narrative inquiry, image based research and application in early childhood education by extending the use of student generated digital images to support inquiry into lived experiences of teaching and learning (Bach, 1998; Clandinin and Connelly, 2001; Packard, Ellison & Sequenzia, 2004; Lemon, 2007). In the two cases presented showing that data collection and analysis of student generated still digital images allows for a teacher-researcher to look more closely at teaching and learning in the early childhood classroom (Schratz & Steiner-Loffler, 1998; Orelana, 1999; Macbeath, Muret & Scratz, 2000; Schratz & Loffler-Anzbock, 2004; Marquez-Zenkov, 2007; Moss, 2007) and provides a closer look at the practices of community including past histories and indoctrination of teaching and learning (Hooks, 1994; Wenger,

1998). As a result presenting how the context of education is substantially enhanced through visual data (Marquez-Zenkov, 2007).

In this chapter the two cases demonstrate how the children, through their visual narratives, have the opportunity to have their voice valued in relation to teaching and learning which allows for making meaning of experiences visually and narratively (Bach, 2007). The visual narrative is akin to digital story telling, and thus a literacy that also means creating meaning, understanding and at the same time being critical (Gee, 2008; New London Group, 1996; Nilsson, 2010; Säljö, 2005).

The case share reminds us that the relationship between text, image and context is a complex one, not least because of the seductiveness of photographs especially when these images are of or generated by children and young people (Grosvenor and Hall, 2012; Holland 2004). The showing and telling of what early childhood children know and think about teaching and learning while valuing and not underestimating their capacity to reflect on their learning through visual narratives and subsequent voice shared (Burnard, 2001; Moss, 2003; Loeffler, 2004; Packard, Ellison & Sequenzia, 2004; Schratz-Hadwich, Walker & Egg, 2004). As Thomson (2008, p. 10) reminds us, children's viewpoints may be marginalized precisely because of their status as children whose lives and images are 'not amenable to straightforward adult readings'. The case shared reinforces that children are capable communicators of their loved experiences through photographs and text and this contribute to the construction of meaning making in relation to their world, and in this case to education. The voice shared honours how others can listen and consider impact on the child, children as a collective, teacher, policy and learning community as a whole. The visual narratives as Huber et al. (2013) embodies such "potential for shaping and extending pedagogy in education" (p. 213).

NOTE

[1] Note that the exact words of the young people are reported here in this dialogue and all visual narratives. The narrative in this case is the students and the images are the teacher. James selected which images he wished to be placed with the narrative.

REFERENCES

Applebee, A. (1978). *The child's concept of story*. Chicago, IL: University of Chicago Press.
Bach, H. (1998). *A visual narrative concerning curriculum, girls, photography etc*. Edmonton, Alberta, Canada: Qual Institute Press.
Bamberg, M. (2012). Narrative analysis. In H. Cooper (Ed.), *APA handbook of research methods in psychology* (pp. 111–130). Washington, DC: American Psychological Association Press.
Brice-Heath, S. (1983). *Ways with words*. New York, NY: Cambridge University Press.
Bruner, J. S. (1983). *Child's talk: Learning to use language*. New York, NY: Norton.
Carr, M. (2001). *Assessment in early childhood settings: Learning stories*. London: Paul Chapman.
Cassell, J., & Ryokai, K. (2001). Making space for voice: Technologies to support children's fantasy and storytelling. *Personal Technologies, 5*(3), 203–224.

Clandinin, D. J., & Connelly, F. M. (1995). *Teachers' professional knowledge landscapes*. New York, NY: Teachers College Press.

Cohen, L., Manion, L., & Morrison, K. (2011). *Research methods in education* (7th ed.). London: Routledge.

Engel, S. (2000). Peeking through the curtain: Narrative as the boundary between secret and known. *Michigan Quarterly Review, XXXIX*(2), 195–208. Retrieved April 16, 2014 from http://quod.lib.umich.edu/cgi/t/text/text-idx?cc=mqr;c=mqr;c=mqrarchive;idno=act2080.0039.203; rgn=main;view=text;xc=1;g=mqrg

Engel, S. (1995). *The stories children tell: Making sense of the narratives of childhood*. New York, NY: W. H. Freeman and Co.

Emde, R., Kubicek, L., & Oppenheim, D. (1997) Imaginative reality observed during early language development. *International Journal of Psychoanalysis, 78*(1), 115–133

Erickson, F. (1996). Going for the zone: Social and cognitive ecology of teacher-student interaction in classroom conversations. In D. Hicks (Ed.), *Discourse, learning and schooling* (pp. 29–62). New York, NY: Cambridge University Press.

Fivush, R., & Hudson, J. A. (Eds.). (1982). *Knowing and remembering in young children*. Cambridge, MA: Cambridge University Press

Freeman, M. (2010). *Hindsight: The promise and peril of looking backward*. New York, NY: Oxford University Press.

Gee, P. (2008). *Social linguistics and literacies: Ideology in discourses*. New York, NY: Routledge.

Grosvenor, I., & Hall, A. (2012). Back to school from a holiday in the slums!: Images, words and inequalities. *Critical Social Policy, 32*(1), 11–30.

Hedberg, N. L., & Westby, C. E. (1993). *Analyzing storytelling skills: Theory to practice*. Tucson, AZ: Communication Skill Builders.

Holland, P. (2004). *Picturing childhood: The myth of the child in popular imagery*. London: I.B. Tauris & Company, Limited.

Kuntay, A., & Ervin-Tripp, S. (1997). Conversational narratives of children: Occasions and structures. *Journal of Narrative and Life History, 7*, 113–120.

Lemon, N. (2008). Looking through the lens of a camera in the early childhood classroom. In J. Moss (Ed.), *Research education: Visually-digitally-spatially* (pp. 21–52). Rotterdam, the Netherlands: Sense Publishers.

Lewis, M. (1993). Self-conscious emotions: Embarrassment, pride, shame and guilt. In M. Lewis & J. Haviland (Eds.), *Handbook of emotion* (pp. 563–573). New York, NY: Guilford Press.

Light, P., & Barnes, P. (1995). Development in drawing. In V. Lee & P. Das Gupta (Eds.), *Children's cognitive and language development*. Oxford: Blackwell/The Open University.

Lilies, B. (1987). Episode organizations and cohesive conjunctives in narratives of children with and without language disorder. *Journal of Speech and Hearing Research, 30*, 185–196.

Marshall, F. (1997, September). Boost your baby's sense of self. *Parents*, 10–12.

Masur, E. F. (1997). Maternal labelling of novel and familiar objects: Implications for children's development of lexical constraints. *Journal of Child Language, 24*(2), 427–439.

Morrow, L. M. (1985). Retelling stories: A strategy for improving young children's comprehension, concept of story structure, and oral language complexity. *The Elementary School Journal, 85*(5), 647–661.

Nelson, K. (1989). *Narratives from the crib*. Cambridge, MA: Harvard University Press.

Nelson, K. (1982). Remembering, forgetting and childhood amnesia. In R. Fivush & J. A. Hudson (Eds.), *Knowing and remembering in young children* (pp. 301–316). Cambridge, MA: Cambridge University Press.

New London Group. (1996). A pedagogy of multiliteracies: Designing social futures. *Harvard Educational Review, 66*, 60–92.

Nilsson, M. (2010). Developing voice in digital storytelling through creativity, narrative and multimodality. *International journal of media, technology and lifelong learning, 6*(2), 148–160.

Rogoff, B. (1990). *Apprenticeship in thinking: Cognitive development in social context*. New York, NY: Oxford University Press.

Rogoff, B. (1998). Cognition as a collaborative process. In D. Kuhn & R. S. Siegler (Eds.), *Handbook of child psychology: Cognition, perception and language* (Vol. 2., pp. 679–744). New York, NY: Wiley.

Rovee-Collier, C., & Gerhardstein, P. (1997). The development of infant memory. In N. Cowan (Ed.), *The development of memory in childhood*. Sussex: Psychology Press.

Säljö, R. (2005). *Lärande och kulturella redskap. Om lärprocesser och det kollektiva minnet*. Stockholm: Norstedts Akademiska Förlag.

Sarbin, T. (2004). The role of imagination in narrative construction. In C. Daiute & C. Lightfoot (Eds.), *Narrative analysis: Studying the development of individual in society* (pp. 5–20). Thousand Oaks, CA: Sage.

Sethi, A., Mischel, W., Aber, J. L., Shoda, Y., & Rodriguez, M. L. (2000) The role of strategic attention deployment in development of self-regulation: Predicting preschoolers' delay of gratification from mother-toddler interactions. *Developmental Psychology, 36*(6), 767–777.

Stadler, M. A., & Ward, G. C. (2005). Supporting the narrative development of young children. *Early Childhood Education Journal, 33*(2), 73–80.

Target, M., & Fonagy, P. (1996). Playing with reality: II. The development of psychic reality from a theoretical perspective. *International Journal of Psychoanalysis, 77*(Pt 3), 459–479.

Thomson, P. (Ed.). (2008). *Doing visual research with children and young people*. London: Routledge.

Tizard, B., & Hodges, J. (1978). The effect of early institutional rearing on the development of eight year-old children. *Journal of Child Psychology and Psychiatry, 19*, 99–118.

Trevarthen, C. (2001). Intrinsic motives for companionship in understanding: Their origin, development and significance for infant mental health. *International Journal of Infant Mental Health, 22*(1–2), 95–131.

Trevarthen, C., Barr, I., Dunlop, A-W., Gjersoe, N., Marwick, H., & Stephen, C. (2003). Supporting a young child's needs for care and affection, shared meaning and a social place. *Review of Childcare and the Development of Children Aged 0–3: Research Evidence, and Implications for Out-of-Home Provision, Insight, 6*. Retrieved April 17, 2014 from http://www.scotland.gov.uk/Resource/Doc/933/0007610.pdf

Vondra, J. I, Shaw, D. S., Swearingen, L., Cohen, M., & Owens. E. B. (2001). Attachment stability and emotional and behavioral regulation from infancy to preschool age. *Developmental Psychopathology, 13*(1), 13–33.

Vygotsky, L. S. (1978). *Mind in society: The development of higher mental processes*. Cambridge, MA: Harvard University Press.

Narelle Lemon
La Trobe University

CHAPTER 8

NARRATIVES BETWEEN CHILDREN

INTRODUCTION

When children participate in narrative talk in an early childhood setting, they engage in an environment that shapes their learning of language, ways of talking and their appropriation of narrative. Children engage in two type of narratives. The first, personal narratives, refer to descriptions of real-life past events and often occur naturally during conversation. The second, fictional narratives, refer to the retellings of familiar stories or self-inspired imaginative stories and tend to occur in an educational setting. Both narrative types produce an interrelated string of clauses and sentences, showing many aspects of language, content form and use (Bruner, 1985; Hughes, McGillivray & Schmidek, 1997). This chapter presents the concept of 'narratives between children' in the creation and co-creation of narratives. It also presents information about the concept of 'artfulness', which is the extent to which the narrator (or child) goes beyond simply recounting the events and captures the attention of the listeners through embellishment of the story. Children who tell elaborate narratives may use interesting words and expressive devices. Children are therefore "storytellers engaged in social events, with all the complications and complex social goals and dynamics that are involved in ay social event" (Bloom, Champion, Katz, Morton & Muldrow, 2000, p. 48). Artfulness is an important tool for educators in the classroom. The role of the educator is therefore to provide spaces to allow narratives between children.

CONSTRUCTING AND CO-CONSTRUCTING NARRATIVES

Bruner (1986) describes narratives as forms of oral discourse that characterise and facilitate culturally determined ways of communicating lived or imagined events to others. As such, narratives are the way in which individuals represent and make sense of past experience, evaluate experiences in the present and plan and anticipate future experiences.

Constructing and conveying a sequence of events by way of a spoken narrative is a common event in children's daily lives. Children have something to say and are experts at being in the moment. They do not live or grow in a 'bubble' but are active participants in their lives. For example, Vivian Paley documented the stories that children tell as part of their daily lives in classrooms. The stories have common themes of questioning fairness and justice, of what transpires with characters in a storybook and the day to day activities children take part in (Paley, 1986, 1993,

2000). All children learn through stories while engaging in play and other activities in early childhood settings. It is therefore important in this book we also explore the concept of narratives between children.

Narratives between children can often take place during pretend and imaginative play. Pretend and imaginative play to allow narratives is considered an important facet of young children's lives in terms of cognition and development (Bergin, 1998). All children engage in narratives, making it important for children to have opportunities to construct and co-construct narrative with other children. The role of the educator is to make spaces for child narratives in the early childhood or school setting.

SHARING STORIES IN EARLY CHILDHOOD AND SCHOOL SETTINGS

Many stories are shared by children in early childhood and school settings. Stories in classrooms are more scripted than home environments as educators engage with large groups of children at once (Dickinson, 1991). When a child is at home that may have informal and less structured conversations with adults with one or a few children. Narratives in school are shared in a different environment and context. At school, the structure of the classroom dictates the types of narratives that are shared in the preschool and the characteristics of the story. Narratives in schools are generally shorter than those shared at home (Dickenson, 1991), however they are also more diverse in form and expose children to a variety of interactions with other children that may not be experienced at home (Dickenson, 2001). Children experience different topics and different narrative structures.

Educators can also engage in narrative sharing during non-structured activities such as meal-time or free play episodes. The role of the educator is to ask genuine questions that can aid the comprehension of the story and help children to become more familiar with diverse narrative practices and traditions (Curenton, 2006).

Sharing (or circle) time has been found to be an important item in a school context in which children are encouraged to share experiences and information with their educators and peers (Cazden, 2001). Children may or may not choose the topic. While the structure of story time may vary across contexts, in general sharing time allows children to share their own narratives. Educators may scaffold children's narrative during this time by asking questions and providing information to clarify and extend children's talk (Michaels, 1991). At time however, educators may have difficulty understanding the stories told to them by students (Cazden, 2001). Unlike parents and family who may have an understanding of the child's experience and be able to provide appropriate scaffolding to help their child's story become coherent, educators are often unaware of the child's experience outside of the school environment (Cazden, 2001; Dicksenson, 1991). It is therefore difficult for educators to provide prompts to facilitate the elaboration of the narrative (Cazden, 2001).

Variation in children's narrative development is also dependent on cultural groups. It is important that educators are also aware of the cultural differences that may exist in children' narrative styles (Michaels, 1991). When an educator listens to a child's narrative, they are expecting a particular type of narrative. Children are expected to tell structured stories based on a central topic with a clear beginning, middle and end (Michaels, 1991). This style is commonly used by middle-class Euro-American parents (Schick & Melzi, 2010). Research suggests however that not all children use this narrative structure. For example, African American children engage in long narratives that are marked by "the juxtaposition of several concrete anecdotes all thematically linked to make an implicit point" (Michaels, 1991 p. 310). Also, the independent narrative of Euro-American children are found to more descriptive and to include more talk about the self than those shared by Chinese children (Wang & Leichtman, 2000). The stories told by Chinese children include more themes of social harmony, social engagement and obedience to authority compared to those told by Euro-American children (Wang & Leichtman, 2000).

Educators who do not understand different structures have difficulty in understanding and scaffolding the narrative for the child (Gee, 1985). In addition to culture, narrative construction between children is also influenced by the structure of the language the children speak. For example, language differ in the number of verbs and adjectives used by the narrator. These linguistic differences influence the structure and content of children's narratives (Minami, 2008).

While the majority of narrative research has focused on adult-child conversations with mothers in the home environment and educators in a school environment, fewer studies have explored the stories children share with one another that are independent of adult scaffolding. Of the studies that have been undertaken, it has been shown that children as young as four years of age are able to adapt the content of their stories to their target audience (Fivush & Hammond, 1990). As children get older, it is also noted that there is developmental progression in children's story telling skills, with greater complexity and structure of the narratives.

There are two main perspectives that have emerged on children stories that have focused on identifying the basic structural elements used by children and the ways in which these are organised to create a cohesive story. The first perspective is grounded in cognitive psychology and based on Propp's (1928) work on Russian folktales and considers stories as series of episodes. Children's narrative abilities are linked to the development of specific cognitive skills and thus posit that children's stories become more complete over time (Stein & Albro, 1997; Stein & Glenn, 1982).

The second perspective is Peterson and McCabe's (1983) high-point analysis. Based on a Labovian perspective, narratives are considered a series of clauses that build up to a climax and ultimately come to a resolution. Scholars adopting this approach consider narratives to be part of children's development of discourse abilities and thus linked to linguistic and conversational gains.

Peterson and McCabe (1983) highlighted in their study qualitative differences in the structure and coherence of the personal narratives told by children during early and middle childhood. They found that while children begin sharing stories during the first years of life, without the support of adult scaffolding children young than four years of age organise information in a temporally disorganised and unsystematic manner, neglecting to include integral information. The onus is therefore placed on the audience to make sense of the story. By the time children are around four and a half years, their stories being to share chronologically organised narratives with temporal linking events.

The most complex narrative genre and the last to develop is fictional narrative. Pre-schoolers' fantasy stories often lack many of the basic structural elements and it is not until around age eight that children share cohesive and sophisticated fictional accounts with complex plots (Hudson & Shapiro, 1991). Thus, over time children become increasingly capable of creating and sharing well-structured narratives through specific developmental trajectories.

The stories between children also differ not only in structure but in content. For example, preschool-age children when sharing wordless picture books make limited references to character's internal states. When they do talk about character emotions they refer to the illustrations. In comparison, during middle childhood, children elaborate on the internal states of characters in storybooks (Berman & Slobin, 1994).

Gender differences related to content have also be shown. Girls' personal narrative are found to be more relational and interpersonal, containing more descriptions, emotions and internal states than the stories shared by boys (Buckner & Fivush, 1998; Ficush et al., 1995). Nicolopoulou (2008) has also found that girls typically preferred a family genre with stories focusing on family in the home setting. By contrast, boys stories adopted a heroic-agnostic genre where there was conflict and an overall lack of harmony.

There is limited investigation on peer interactions in early childhood settings, especially with very young children. This is surprising considering that peer interactions play an integral role in children's everyday lives from early childhood onwards. We know that children as young as four engage in peer narratives (Kyratzis & Ervin-Tripp, 1999; Umiker-Sebeok, 1979). Talk between children provides opportunities to "actively negotiate meanings and relationships related to their local peer culture, creating a web of cultural tools and possible words unique to childhood" (Blum-Kulka, Huck-Taglich & Avni, 2004, p. 308).

Stories told with peers contain more performance features to engage the audience (such as repetition). Young children also become active listeners to the narrator, requesting orienting information, spontaneously providing information and generally serving to improve the coherence of the narratives (Nicolopoulou & Richer, 2004). The sharing of narratives with peers therefore facilitates children's development of the diverse pragmatic and discursive skills essential to story telling.

ARTFULNESS

One way for an educator to explore stories between children is by exploring narratives for the concept of artfulness. Artfulness can be used as a tool for analysis. Artfulness encompasses the creative, imaginative, and joyful elements of stories that are often missed in objective measures of narratives. Artfulness is also known in the literature as "sparkle" (Peterson & McCabe, 1983), "story quality" (Gutierrez-Clellen & DeCurtis, 2001; McFadden & Gilliam, 1986) and "expressive elaboration" (Ukrainetz et al., 2005). According to Peterson and McCabe (1983, p. 1), artfulness represents the "freshness, the creativity, the unpredictability, the amusement" of stories. Artfulness therefore makes children's narratives interesting, alive and enjoyable. Educators can analyse narratives in such a manner.

Artfulness emerges not only from the child but the environment of the child. Within the socio-cultural context in which the child exists, the child is influenced by other children, adults, environments and circumstances that continually change. The child's creativity for narratives is therefore developed through the child's unique and personal perspective (Csikszentmihalyi, 1996; Rinaldi, 2006; Rogoff, 2003). The words that children choose and their narrative styles are products of the child's world as are the way the child interacts with the listener. All of these differ with each child.

The documentation and assessment of artfulness in children's narrative may provide a complete picture of the unique and individual aspects of children's expressive elements. While most studies of artfulness and young children have been confined to school rather than preschool age children (Newman & McGregor, 2006) there is much potential for artfulness with all children. Since narratives occur as a normal part of social conversations, the narratives children tell with each other provide an ecologically valid context for exploring children's language abilities compared to traditional assessment of language competence (Paul & Smith, 1993). Narratives can therefore represent a culturally sensitive assessment tool that captures subtleties of language content form (Price, Roberts & Jackson, 2006) and allow the educator to understand the meaning-making of the child. Construction of narratives between children provides examples of shared meaning-making between children and how they can support one another in their creation of meaning.

There are three notable studies in artfulness that are worth mentioning. The first is a study by Ukrainetz et al. (2005) that examined the artful performance of fictional narratives in 293 children between the aged five and twelve years. Findings revealed that children created more elaborate and artful stories with age. The older the child, the more expressive elements were used. The research team also found that children within and across age range groups demonstrated diverse patterns of acquisition of 13 types of expressive elaboration explored. The authors also stated that accounting for the many ways in which narratives can be demonstrated in 'story art', allows for a more multifaceted approach to narrative assessment.

In the second study, Ukrainetz and Gillam (2009) studied artfulness in the fictional narratives of 48 pairs of children (96 children took part). The pairs consisted of a child with typical language and a child with language impairment.

Children identified as having language impairment produced significantly fewer elements of artfulness in their narratives compared to children with typical language. The study makes an essential contribution toward understanding the importance of artfulness as an informative index of narrative skill among school-age children.

The final study worth mentioning (Glenn-Applegate, Breit-Smith, Justice & Piasta, 2010) explored the artfulness of 43 children aged between 3 years, 6 months to 4 years, 11 months. Results indicated that narrative artfulness was positively and uniquely associated with children's general language performance. Children who produced more artful narratives tended to produce narratives that were more lexically diverse. Young children also used a lot of adverbs. Humour was used as an element of the stories by 40% of children. Overall, these three studies make an essential contribution to understanding the importance of artfulness as an informative index of narrative skill. It allows a tool for educators to implement.

The role of the educator in exploring artfulness between children in the classroom is important. Educators in high-quality preschool programs support the understanding and use of language through focusing on the past, future or imaginary in stories with decontextualized language. Decontextualized language is defined as language that is context-free and autonomous. It is not grounded in any immediate context of time or situation and does not rely on observation or an immediate physical experience. Decontextualized language emerges often in the context of imaginative play and provides opportunities for children to engage in communication with and express meaning to other children. Copple and Bredekamp (2009) have also found that the use of decontextualized language helps children to make meaning from printed texts. Thus it is an important tool to enhance future literacy.

Educators can use measures of macrostructures and microstructures when analysing children's narrative between one another for artfulness (Hughes et al., 1997). The macrostructure of a narrative refers to the general schema to which a narrative adheres. This could include references to story grammar (such as the setting of time) and character personality features and internal states (Hedberg & Stoel-Gammon, 1986; Stein & Glenn, 1979). Microstructure reflects the linguistic structure children use when conveying a story. These could include the use of cohesive devices (words and clauses that tie sentences together), clauses (groups of words with a subject and predicate) and word choice (richness of vocabulary).

Some aspects of artfulness, such as emphasis, are more readily available during oral story telling, when one or more people serve as an audience. Young children who create stories between one another can have opportunity to show their artfulness by selecting words together, building suspense and adding personal flavour to affect stories. When the children work together they can apply the expressive elements they know across different genres of narrative discourse, including both personal accounts of real-life events and imaginative stories.

IMPLEMENTING ARTFULNESS

One tool educators can use to assess artfulness is to allow children to construct meaning about wordless picture books (used as a narrative elicitation prompt. One book that may be useful is the picture book *Frog, Where Are You?* (Mayer, 1969). Through pictures alone, the book tells the story of a boy who loses his pet frog and with the help of his dog, searches for the frog in the forest. The book allows young children to create a coherent narrative by way of integrating information across pages of pictures, thus resembling typical narrative retellings used to measure reading comprehension activities who might read in a conventional sense.

In the study by Glenn-Applegate, Breit-Smith, Justice and Piasta (2010), engaged with their text in their artfulness studies with young children. The narrative elicitation took place in a quiet area in the school. The child was informed of the story telling task and they could create their own story based on the pictures in the book. The entire process was videotaped to allow the research to review the narration. Each narrative was then analysed using a coding scheme adapted from the work of Ukrainetz and Gillam (2009) and Ukrainetz et al. (2005) to identify elements of artfulness. These included theme, coda, expression, interesting modifiers, interjections, humour beyond the page and stress.

In recent data I have collected on children's stories in a kindergarten, instead of using a published picture book, I created my own book of photos from a visit to a park. The children were asked to share a story based on the pictures they were viewing. Examples of the photos (Figures 27 and 28) are shared below.

Figure 27. Dog in park with tennis ball.

Figure 28. Playground equipment.

The narratives were digitally recorded and then coded for similar features identified by Glenn-Applegate, Breit-Smith, Justice & Piasta (2010). I was particularly interested in the use of adverbs and adjectives by the child. I coded the transcripts looking for frequencies of:

- Relationships
- Adjectives
- Adverbs
- Interjections
- Repetitions
- Internal states
- Dialogue
- Humour
- Beyond the page
- Stress

Every time one of these elements was mentioned, I would make a note on my transcript and frequency counts. Children appeared to use adjectives and adverbs frequently in their narration. Children would often talk about their internal stage in relation to the pictures. A smaller group of children attempted humour in the telling of the narrative.

After the research I was able to share the findings with the kindergarten teacher. She was amazed at the extent to which children were active users of adjectives and adverbs. The artfulness helped inform her future planning of learning experiences for the children and also provided the opportunity for documentation of the children's learning.

The role of the educator is vital in the development of artfulness in an early childhood or school setting. By allowing spaces in the education setting for children to share narratives between each other and with the educator, children are given opportunities to extend their own narrative understanding. The educator can also model the use of artful language by emphasising descriptive words and adding stress. For example. "We're going to catch a *big* one and *we're* not scared", Rosen & Oxenbury, 2003).

Thoughtful consideration is needed of narrative between children can be constructive and gainful for all. It can lead to better practice and renewed rigour for understanding the meaning making children construct. Recognising artfulness as a significant and important element of narratives between children allows new understanding of children language and culture. The approach is respectful of the narratives that children tell.

CONCLUSION

By sharing narratives with others, children can acquire the basic skills needed to produce a narrative in the form of a story that is valued in their community. Narrative is a form of discourse that is frequently used, with, around and between children across societies. Cultural norms are embedded in the manner in which stories are shared and thus an understanding by the educator or educator is necessary. It is essential that educators understand the cultural backgrounds of their students to ensure that they build on the practices of narration that children bring to the classroom. Artfulness is one technique to explore the narratives between children. It encompasses the creative, imaginative and joyful elements of narratives. Educators can document and assess the artfulness in narratives between children to gain insights into the children's world and language development. The approach is respectful of children and provides opportunities for stories of children to be observed in every day settings in early childhood and school settings. The final chapter of the book will explore narratives without children.

REFERENCES

Bergin, D. (1998). Stages of play development. In D. Bergen (Ed.), *Readings from play as a medium for learning and development* (pp. 71–93). Olney, MD: Association for Childhood Education International.

Berman, R. A., & Slobin, D. I. (1994). *Relating events in narrative: A crosslinguistic developmental study*. Hillsdale, NJ: Erlbaum.

Bloom, D., Champion, T., Katz, L., Morton, M. B., & Muldrow, R. (2000). Spoken and written narrative development: African American preschoolers as storytellers and storymakers. In J. L. Harris, A. G. Kamhi, & K. E. Pollock (Eds.), *Literacy in African American communities* (pp. 45–76). Mahwah, NJ: Erlbaum.

Blum-Kulka, S., Huck-Taglicht, D., & Avni, H. (2004). The social and discursive spectrum of peer talk. *Discourse Studies, 6*, 307–328.

Bruner, J. (1985). Models of the learner. *Educational Researcher, 14*(6), 5–8.

Bruner, J. (1986). *Actual minds, possible worlds*. Cambridge, MA: Harvard University Press.

Buckner, J. P., & Fivush, R. (1998). Gender and self in children's autobiographical narratives. *Applied Cognitive Psychology, 12*, 407–429.

Cazden, C. B. (2001). *Classroom discourse: The language of teaching and learning* (2nd ed.). Westport, CT: Heinemann.

Copple, C., & Bredekamp, S. (Eds.). (2009). *Developmentally appropriate practice in early childhood programs* (3rd ed.). Washington, DC: National Association for the Education of Young Children.

Csikszentmihalyi, M. (1996). *Creativity: Flow and the psychology of discovery and invention.* New York, NY: Harper Collins.

Curenton, S. M. (2006). Oral storytelling: A cultural art that promotes school readiness. *Young Children, 61*, 78–89.

Dickinson, D. K. (1991). Teacher agenda and setting: Constraints on conversation in preschools. In A. McCabe & C. Peterson (Eds.), *Developing narrative structure* (pp. 255–301). Hillsdale, NJ: Erlbaum.

Dickinson, D. K. (2001). Book reading in preschool classrooms: Is recommended practice common? In D. K. Dickinson & P. O. Tabors (Eds.), *Beginning literacy with language: Young children learning at home and school* (pp. 175–203). Baltimore, MD: Brookes.

Fivush, R., Haden, C., & Adam, S. (1995). Structure and coherence of preschoolers' personal narratives over time: Implications for childhood amnesia. *Journal of Experimental Child Psychology, 60*(1), 32–56.

Fivush, R., & Hammond, N. (1990). Autobiographical memory across the preschool years: Toward reconceptualising childhood amnesia. In R. Fivush & J. Hudson (Eds.), *Knowing and remembering in young children* (pp. 223–248). New York, NY: Cambridge University Press.

Gee, J. P. (1985). The narrativization of experience in the oral style. *Journal of Education, 167*(1), 9–35.

Glenn-Applegate, K., Breit-Smith, A., Justice, L. M., & Piasta, S. B. (2010) Artfulness in young children's spoken narratives. *Early Education and Development, 21*(3), 468–493.

Gutiérrez-Clellen, V. F., & DeCurtis, L. (2001). Examining the quality of children's stories: Clinical applications. *Seminars in Speech and Language, 22*(1), 79–89.

Hedberg, N. L., & Stoel-Gammon, C. (1986). Narrative analysis: Clinical procedures. *Topics in Language Disorders, 7*(1), 58–69.

Hudson, J. A., & Shapiro, L. R. (1991). From knowing to telling: The development of children's scripts, stories, and personal narratives. In A. McCabe & C. Peterson (Eds.), *Developing narrative structure* (pp. 89–136). Hillsdale, NJ: Erlbaum.

Hughes, D., McGillivray, L., & Schmidek, M. (1997). *Guide to narrative language: Procedures for assessment.* Eau Claire, WI: Thinking Publications.

Kyratzis, A., & Ervin-Tripp, S. (1999). The development of discourse markers in peer interaction. *Journal of Pragmatics, 31*, 1321–1338.

McFadden, T. U., & Gillam, R. B. (1996). An examination of the quality of narratives produced by children with language disorders. *Language, Speech, and Hearing Services in Schools, 27*, 48–56.

Mayer, M. (1969). *Frog, where are you?* New York, NY: Dial Books for Young Readers.

Michaels, S. (1991). The dismantling of narrative. In A. McCabe & C. Peterson (Eds.), *Developing narrative structure* (pp. 303–351). Hillsdale, NJ: Erlbaum.

Minami, M. (2008). Telling good stories in different languages: Bilingual children's styles of story construction and their linguistic and educational implications. *Narrative Inquiry, 18*(1), 83–110.

Newman, R. M., & McGregor, K. K. (2006). Teachers and laypersons discern quality differences between narratives produced by children with or without SLI. *Journal of Speech, Language, and Hearing Research, 49*, 1022–1036.

Nicolopoulou, A., & Richner, E. S. (2004). When your powers combine, I am Captain Planet: The developmental significance of individual- and group-authored stories by preschoolers. *Discourse Studies, 6*, 347–371.

Paley, V. G. (1986). *Boys and girls: Superheroes in the doll corner.* Chicago, IL: University of Chicago Press.

Paley, V. G. (1993). *You can't say you can't play.* Cambridge, MA: Harvard University Press.

Paley, V. G. (2000). *White teacher.* Cambridge, MA: Harvard University Press.

Paul, R., & Smith, R. L. (1993). Narrative skills in 4-year-olds with normal, impaired, and late-developing language. *Journal of Speech and Hearing Research, 36*, 592–598.

Peterson, C., & McCabe, A. (1983). *Developmental psycholinguistics: Three ways of looking at a child's narrative.* New York, NY: Plenum Press.

Pinar, W. (2004). *What is curriculum theory?* Mahwah, NJ: Erlbaum.

Price, J. R., Roberts, J. E., & Jackson, S. C. (2006). Structural development of the fictional narratives of African American preschoolers. *Language, Speech, and Hearing Services in Schools, 37,* 178–190.

Propp, V. I. (1968). *Morphology of the folktale* (2nd ed.). Austin, TX: University of Texas Press. (Original work published 1928)

Rinaldi, C. (2006). *In dialogue with Reggio Emilia: Listening, researching and learning.* New York, NY: Routledge.

Rogoff, B. (2003). *The cultural nature of human development.* New York, NY: Oxford University Press.

Rosen, M., & Oxenbury, H. (2003). *We're going on a bear hunt.* New York, NY: Little Simon.

Schick, A., & Melzi, G. (2010) The development of children's oral narratives across contexts. *Early Education and Development, 21*(3), 293–317.

Stein, N. L., & Albro, E. R. (1997). Building complexity and coherence: Children's use of goal-structured knowledge in telling stories. In M. Bamberg (Ed.), *Narrative development: Six approaches* (pp. 5–44). Mahwah, NJ: Erlbaum.

Stein, N. L., & Glenn, C. G. (1979). An analysis of story comprehension in elementary school children. In R. O. Freedle (Ed.), *New directions in discourse processing* (pp. 53–120). Norwood, NJ: Ablex.

Ukrainetz, T. A., & Gillam, R. B. (2009). The expressive elaboration of imaginative narratives by children with specific language impairment. *Journal of Speech, Language, and Hearing Research, 52,* 883–898.

Ukrainetz, T. A., Justice, L. M., Kaderavek, J. N., Eisenberg, S. L., Gillam, R. B., & Harm, H. M. (2005). The development of expressive elaboration in fictional narratives. *Journal of Speech, Language, and Hearing Research, 48,* 1363–1377.

Umiker-Sebeok, D. J. (1979). Preschool children's intraconversational narratives. *Journal of Child Language, 6*(1), 91–109.

Wang, Q., & Leichtman, M. D. (2000). Same beginnings, different stories: A comparison of American and Chinese children's narratives. *Child Development, 71,* 1329–1346.

Susanne Garvis
University of Gothenburg

117

NARRATIVE WITHOUT CHILDREN

INTRODUCTION

Story telling and narratives without children have a strong history in education. There is a significant amount of research carried out that represent narratives of children provided by educators. As Henderson, Meier and Perry (2004) share, "these teacher research studies are grounded in the daily lives of children and based on the insights of the teachers or caregivers who work with them" (p. 94). In working this way we are reminded that:

> The teacher examines a problem from many perspectives, collects and interprets data, and reflects on the findings. Thus teacher research in early childhood education provides unique insider perspectives on real issues in early care and education settings. (Henderson, Meier & Perry, 2004, p. 94)

The way in which researchers perceive childhood and the status of children in society and the community influences how children and childhood is understood (Punch, 2002). This is reinforced by Sanborn & Giardino (2014) who invited us to consider the following:

> The child's social environment is populated with adults and other children. What we are learning is that these interactions can have a tremendous impact on children and their development… Every interaction our children have, whether with a parent, teacher, caregiver, or even a peer could have a noticeable impact. (Sanborn & Giardino, 2014, para 1)

In her work in early childhood, Punch (2002) explores different methodological approaches to research with and on children. She suggests that "one way of researching a diversity of childhoods and taking into account children's varied social competencies and life experiences is to use a range of different methods and techniques" (p. 322). This has certainly been reiterated throughout this book. When considering how to represent research on children it must be remembered that it is potentially different from research with adults "mainly because of adult perceptions of children and children's marginalized position in adult society but least often because children are inherently different" (Punch, 2002, p. 321).

This chapter explores a case of teachers being researchers about young children to impact their practice, to investigate a problem and to enact reflective practice. Literature is explored that highlights how being a teacher-researcher can enhance professional learning. An exploration of literature on photography as a way to research practice is also explored. Following these discussions, one case is presented that is located within the early year setting whereby visual narrative and image based methods have been accessed to create narratives without children about learning spaces.

CONSIDERATION OF PHOTOGRAPHY IN THE LEARNING ENVIRONMENT

Type 'digital photography in the classroom' into your search engine and numerous sites appear with suggestions such as making books, creating stories through photos, making labels and using photos to show instructions visually. In addition, there are numerous suggestions for teachers about using a digital camera to photograph children on excursions, recording special theme days, producing displays for the classroom, and providing images to promote school and classroom practice. Research sites also appear, which focus on girls' education (Bach, 1998) and inclusive curriculum practice (Carrington & Holm, 2005; Moss & Hay, 2004). However, what is overlooked is the use of still digital photography in the classroom as a reflective tool that enables learners to share their learning stories (Carr, 2001) in the form of visual narratives (Bach, 1998; Clandinin & Connelly, 2000; Moss, 2003).

With the emergence of digital photography, cameras that require film are no longer practical for schools (Van House et al., 2004). Digital technology allows the user to take a photo, see immediately if it needs to be retaken, delete if necessary, and print to a printer or save directly to a computer. No extra expense is involved once the full capacity of photos is taken – simply download, delete and start again. Gone is the fear of the film being loaded incorrectly or of disappointing results. Importantly, digital cameras are now recognized as a resource for teaching in the 21st century classroom (Ewald & Lightfoot, 2001; Eber, 2002; Hamilton, 2004). The digital camera can be available when needed and readily used as a part of the daily curriculum. The use of the digital camera also addresses the research concerns of Inkpen (2001) and Sharpies (2002) who argue that the smaller and less destructive the device, the more chance it stands of becoming a life-long learning tool, anywhere and anytime.

For educators, the digital camera is a tool that allows accessible technology to enter the classroom and assume a key role in the enactment of curriculum. In the twenty first century, curriculum documents for schools are stipulating more integrated use of technology. Technology is no longer a separate subject run by a specialist teacher but embodies interdisciplinary knowledge, skills and behaviours that must be applied to all subjects. With this comes the challenge for teachers to use technology and to embed technology across the curriculum. But as Swan et al. (2005) attest, many teachers are struggling to integrate the use of technology.

PHOTOGRAPHY AS A LANGUAGE OF TEACHER INQUIRY

Using photography as a tool for inquiry is not new (Roxburgh & Kasunic, 2005). Since the 1800s photography has been used for understanding the social world in history, critical sociology, ethnography, and anthropology. Regardless of the place, time and use photography relies heavily on models of representation that are affected by attitudes and values found in realism (Berger & Mohr, 1982). Photography when established as a key element of teacher research and teacher inquiry has the potential to make visible teacher questions, to capture children's learning, and to challenge and highlight discrepancies between theory and practice (Moran & Tegano, 2005). It is through the process of looking, evaluating, questioning, studying, and rearranging photographs that reflective and reflexive thinking about one's own practice and learning (Miles & Kaplan, 2005) is foregrounded.

As early as 1970 Rob Walker and his colleagues were researching classroom practice through photography. Photographs were taken automatically at "intervals of two seconds and the film was then synchronized with sound, using similar principles to tape-slide presentation" (Walker & Adelman, 1975, p. 135). These presentations were used with the aim of developing teachers' observational skills, to promote changed teacher action in their classrooms.

The possibilities of using photographs to provide insights into learning and pedagogy that may assist in changing teacher pedagogy and practices have been highlighted in recent literature (Grauer, Irwin, Cosson & Wilson, 2001; Chronaki & Jess, 2002; Ainscow et al., 2004; Daniels, 2004; Schratz-Hadwich, Walker & Egg, 2004; Moran & Tegano, 2005; Miles & Kaplan, 2005). As the body of literature suggests, photographs can provide an innovative approach to practice and research, for example, understanding diversity and supporting new learning relationships and knowledge. Photographs can also be used to elicit a more holistic self-evaluation process, providing visual records that trigger reflection, diverse interpretations and discussions of memory. Schratz-Hadwich, Walker and Egg (2004) reiterate that photographic method can provide opportunities for "reflective practice overtime, not just reflective practice in action as that [in itself] doesn't allow for more logical analysis of practice" (p. 4). Reflective practice is likewise highlighted in the work of Worden (2003). He argues that the research process of seeing the world through photographs encourages reflection-in-action (Schön, 1987), thus is an ideal reflective tool. The context of the visual does not mean anything until reflection takes place.

A further example of research which used digitised images as a source to prompt reflection is the research of Grauer et al. (2001) or Lemon (2008). In an artist and teacher partnership through the program 'Learning through the Arts' in British Columbia, teachers and artists discussed the use of photographs as professional development with arts teachers. The study highlights photo elicitation as a collaborative research method and demonstrates how forms of image based analysis by groups of researchers, teachers and artists can be developed. Through who, what, and why questions designed to trigger reflective thinking for both teachers and their students, the focus and contribution of visual images was shown to enhance deeper thinking results. The study of Grauer et al. (2001) discussed beliefs about teaching and learning, particularly the relationship between teacher experiences and their emergent classroom practice. Of interest was the researchers' observation that teachers became more involved in the classroom activities when the camera was present, whilst the children seemed oblivious to the camera's presence. This raises questions such as: *How do teachers see themselves when photographed in practice? Are they more self-conscious than children? How does this impact on naturalistic inquiry?*

One of the stated benefits to teachers is the use of photographs as part of their professional learning, allowing the sharing of experiences in ways not possible through narrative descriptions which are limited to words. Walker and Adelman (1975) believe that recording the context through the visual provides teachers with material for developing deeper understanding through the discussion of their images. Photographs "catch something quite unlike what we think we see and yet enough like it to be recognizable and useful" (Walker & Adelman, 1975, p. 131). Sequences of photographs can be a record of the physical environment of a classroom, examples of children's work, or what 'working' actually looks like. Photographs can serve multiple purposes and may include:

> a record of aggravation and/or dissolution; a child's attempt to attract attention; joy and excitement; and be a useful context for reflection on a lesson. Significantly, interpretation of photographs can lead to alternative interpretations and impact on professional practice. (Walker & Adelman, 1975)

Daniels (2004) supports the linking of reflective practice and photographs as "pedagogical tools that provide deeper insight" (p. 1). Through photographs, she states, "I could gain a better understanding of their [children's] visibility, strengths and potential within the community" (Daniels, 2004, p. 3).

Carr's (1998; 2001) significant research on Learning Stories in the early childhood context provides useful insights for educational researchers interested in the application of photography in the design of educational research. Carr's work demonstrates how photographs generated by the teacher are evidence of student learning. In Carr's work, photographs are generated by the teacher and do not include a student narrative. Her construct of Learning Stories is a strong demonstrated example of digital photographs and text being used together in the early childhood classroom for reflection purposes, albeit with an explicit assessment focus.

The work of Moran and Tegano (2005) in the preschool and early childhood classroom, reveals how photographs can be used to promote systematic inquiry of professional practice with three functional applications – the representational, meditational and epistemological. Moran and Tegano refer to teacher inquirers being classroom researchers who engage in cyclic studies of learning in context and use tools such as cameras and photographs to help make teaching and learning visible. Implicit in their functional application is a focus on reflective practice. Using this method they found that:

> …teachers can learn to observe carefully, screening out non seminal information as they develop discernment, judgment and decision-making skills' and that teachers can 'represent, examine and communicate emerging understandings with others and with self. (Moran & Tegano, 2005, p. 2)

REFLECTIVE PRACTICE AND IMAGES GENERATED BY CHILDREN

Observation of children coupled with teachers' reflective practice provides opportunities to reorganize pedagogy and subsequently impact children's learning experiences. It is the opportunity to engage with children's reflection and/or voice to augment teachers' reflective practices that is, however, often overlooked. Teachers' reflective practice is seldom informed by the students' reflective lens (Lemon, 2007). As Hedy Bach (1998) writes:

> I learned how camera works can evoke different emotions and stories of possibilities and of impossibility. I began to see how photography was embodied in my story and how it re/presents a sensory form of knowing. I was situated within a story and photography that pressed me to question my practices by looking. (p. 15)

Bach's (1998) use of student generated photographs and subsequent visual narratives, coupled with teacher inquiry and reflective practice, have provided a model and framework for this study. Other studies have addressed one of these aspects, but very few have synthesized student generated photographs, visual narratives, teacher inquiry and reflective practice. Although Hedy Bach worked with adolescent women, many of her principles are applicable to the early childhood classroom. Through working with the participants in her study, Bach (1998) reports:

> ...narrative knowing generated from our experiences and understanding of the body as a site of meaning-making [enables connections to be made outside-in and inside-out, thereby providing the means to] dig into our interior lives, providing a holistic approach. (pp. vii–viii)

As Clandinin and Connelly (1994) acknowledge, personal experience method is a way to maintain questioning, self-evaluation, intimacy, friendship, familiarity and to make the private public. Most importantly for this study, Bach's work establishes a framework for examining one's teaching practice as being embodied. The student produced images used in conjunction with a reflective teacher stance relied on the power that photographs have to give students and teachers a voice about learning spaces, experiences and educational institutions (Moss, 2008). As Grauer et al. (2001) and Ainscow et al. (2004) attest the use of photographs is likely to be very challenging, and success is dependent on the quality of relationships between learners and teachers. From another stance, Packard, Ellison and Sequenzia (2004) mention the possibilities and excitement attached to the idea of using photographs in the context of university communities.

CHILD GENERATED IMAGES—PHOTOGRAPHS FOR REFLECTION

Children can take photographs, annotate them with captions or titles, use them in journals, or engage with them during interviews or conversations as a stimulus for reflection. In using the camera, the children are telling their stories by drawing on the language of the images to show their story (Walker & Adelman, 1975; Fasoli, 2003; Ellum, 2005; Ramella & Olmos, 2005). Children's images elicit their perspectives (Burnard, 2001; Moss, 2003; Packard, Ellison & Sequenzia, 2004) and can be used to gain understanding about significant issues in a child's or an adolescent's life, especially when the 'participants take the photo themselves' (Packard, Ellison & Sequenzia, 2004, p. 3).

The term 'photo evaluation' (Schratz-Hadwich, Walker & Egg, 2004), describes the method as a unique and feasible tool to use in evaluation and research with children, as it shows relevant data quickly. Photo evaluation involves children in the research and self-evaluation process. It can add richness to the review of events by enabling adults to understand and learn about the children, and the teacher's enacted curriculum and pedagogy.

Imaged-based techniques in research allow for the representation of what children know, feel and think about their learning (Burnard, 2001), and provide strong and powerful ways of accessing thinking (Schratz-Hadwich et al., 2004). Pam Burnard's study on student generated images posed the question *What is going on?* to trigger responses from the student participants. Burnard indicated that the question stimulated 'richly informative' responses when students were provided with concrete photographs compared with student participants in other studies who were simply asked to consider the question *Who am I?* when they took photographs of their experiences (Ramella & Olmos, 2005).

Photo elicitation has been commonly used with children. Images, not necessarily taken by the children themselves, have been used as a trigger or stimulus for an interview (Collier, 1967; Harper, 1998; Grauer, Irwin, Cosson & Wilson, 2001; Pink, 2001; Warren, 2002). Loeffler (2004) worked with 18–21 year-old university outdoor education students and used photo elicitation interviews as a tool for reflection. In the study the researcher became the "listener as the subject interpreted the images and their meaning" (p. 1). Packard, Ellison and Sequenzia (2004) worked with 14 adolescent girls aged between 13 and 19 years in Urbantown, Massachusetts and found that using photos in the interviews with the girls provided 'additional insights' into their culture, community and what was important to them, including their hopes, fears and reminders of the past. Photo elicitation can be understood as a process where photos are "containers in which many things can be stored; they can hold details, memories, emotions, and meanings" (Loeffler, 2004, p. 1), thus allowing for moments to be captured, stored and shared later.

By contrast, photo novella (Wang & Burris, 1994) links closely with photo interviewing and results in the creation of photo stories. In this approach), children or other participants are given the camera and later their photographs are used with the researcher for reflection purposes. Similar to reflexive photography (Ziller, 1990; Harrington & Lindy, 1998; Berman et al., 2001), photo novella has been reported as promoting deeper levels of reflective thinking than interviews alone. Photo stories have also been explored in the work of Daniel Meadows (2006) and Louisa Ellum

(2005). In these studies digital photographs were used in a tale that featured a story of story tellers telling a story in their own words. Meadows' work focuses on photos as "reposits for memory" (p. 90) in which the focus is on one element and the sharing of a story that the teller wishes to tell.

The advantages of using photography as a medium for reflection have been reported extensively in the aforementioned studies. These advantages resonate in the words of Walker and Adelman (1975, p. 129) when they say, "[photographs] recreate incidents more vividly than narrative description...you become aware of the different realities retained and created by the different techniques". Bach (1998), in her visual narrative study of adolescent girls, linked photographs with curriculum to help understand lived experiences and issues important to the participants. In doing this, Bach addressed student generated photographs to awaken and celebrate thinking positions through the gaps and possibilities that emerged.

Imaged based research has limitless potential for educational purposes with children and adults (Harper, 1998; Prosser, 1998) and it is currently undervalued (Lemon, 2007; 2008). Research shows that in working with children and adolescents photos are a source for reflection and that multiple outcomes can be achieved. This chapter takes up one case whereby photo self elicitation as a way to promote the generation of images and text that are meaningful to early childhood children, and likewise points to the multiple outcomes of enhanced learner identity, student voice and learner perspectives. This chapter presents a case where the educator has generated visual narratives on and about children but without their input, this is very different to the cases presented in Chapter 7 of this book and offers a different perspective and approach.

A CASE OF INVESTIGATING YOUNG CHILDREN TO INVESTIGATE A PROBLEM

In this section of the chapter teacher generated images taken of children in their learning environment are presented. The narrative provided by the teacher captures the voice of the children in regards to a conversation or comment made at the time that the image(s) was generated. Some notes are made about observations in regards to learning, skills or attitudes. The visual narrative generated is about the children.

This case introduces a longitudinal research project that aimed to investigate school readiness of young children in an educational setting located in Melbourne, Australia. In August 2011 the Department of Education and Early Childhood Development (DEECD) in the state of Victoria was pressuring Mill Park Heights Primary School to abandon its two-year prep program (four- to six-year-olds), saying it breaches department policy. It was reported that:

> ...parents are increasingly demanding their children begin primary school before they are ready, forcing many to repeat prep and prompting the state's largest primary school to offer a two-year prep program to deal with the influx of immature children. (Gough, 2011, para 1)

In Australia preparatory, or prep, government school programs are traditionally one year. Some students may repeat the prep year if they are viewed as not ready for the next stages of schooling. Mill Park Heights Primary School identified a rise in this need to occur especially after noting a consistent pattern of young children being sent to school too early due to "financially burdened parents [reporting] the cost of childcare and kindergarten, and the prospect of another year out of the workforce are factors in requesting their children start school early" (Gough, 2011, para 2). This was seen as a significant issue and to problem solve a two year prep program was developed and piloted a two-year prep program.

By December 2011 the program was being seen by DEECD as a pilot that may go statewide in the future. In 2012 the school had 2 two-year prep program classes, each with 18 children. The students wore the same uniform as other prep students to feel a part of the school community. The parents paid the same fees as per a prep program. And the overall timetable was designed as other prep classes. The only difference was that curriculum design was centred more on play based curriculum that did not feature significantly in the prep program nor subsequent grade levels. It is expected that not all of these children will stay in Prep for two years, but they will have the option to be included if not deemed ready to move to the next stages of schooling.

The future of this two-year prep program was viewed as potential for rich study as part of the financial viability of early year education in the state of Victoria's and potentially nationally. As a part of the research design an evaluation for its effectiveness at multiple levels was deemed important. This was designed as a long term commitment—to follow through at least one or several cohorts of children over a period of four to five years. Key aspects to be investigated were, the children's:

- Academic readiness
- Social readiness
- Emotional readiness

The project also saw it as important to investigate the financial sustainability of the program (e.g., cost effectiveness if there is no future need for remediation for these students). Thirdly, the program itself would be evaluated over time with guiding questions of – what's working and what isn't? It was viewed by the research team that parents', teachers' and the school administration's voices and perspectives would heard in the evaluation. Children's voices was also seen as important however not a key focus of the study. This is where narratives on children are highlighted as assessment reports written by teachers, work samples completed by children by analysed by adults, observation of children in the learning environment, and school reporting data formed the majority of the narratives presented. The research questions generated included:

- Why did the school set up the two-year prep program (and its predecessor)?
- How were the children selected by the school for the two-year prep program?
- Why did the parents choose the two-year prep program?

- Was there sufficient interest in the program by parents to form sufficient groups?
- What is the level of parental support for the program?
- What are the expectations and understandings of the program by parents, teachers and children?
- What is each child's prep entry assessment data telling us about their academic readiness?
- How are the children coping in the program?

This case is presented as an example of how a project has been established that will generate narratives on children. It sees a variety of data collection approaches that share perspectives from researcher, teacher, parents, and policy makers. Although the data sources collected did not specifically set out to investigate narratives with children, I as one of the research team did seek permission to have students generate their own visual narratives about what was important to them at school. This alternative use of data is explored in Chapter 7. However, when thinking about narratives on children, it is possible to work with creative methodologies to generate narratives on children that still include them as participants.

This case thus builds on learning the work of image based methods, learning stories (Carr, 2001), and observation methods. All these digital still photographs are researcher generated. Interspersed is the voice of the researcher as observer, and the young children and as they participated in the learning of their classroom.

A sample is shared and not the full transcript or observation. The tale begins…

The class is sitting on the floor in a circle (see Figure 29). Legs are crossed by most students although there is the occasional student slouching, with their body draped over themselves. One girl [Bella, a small girl with glasses) has removed herself from the circle and is lying on an old armchair just on the boarder of the

Figure 29. Class sitting on the floor.

127

rest of her classmates. Two teachers are sitting with the students in the circle, each opposite one another on low chairs as so there height is not too far above the students sitting on the floor. Each student is introduced to Lyn and Narelle [researchers]. They say hello collectively to them both. Then they are asked to say their name and share something they like. The sharing reinforces students to speak loudly and to communicate their like. The teacher encourages louder voices. Some students do not want to share and just look at the teacher without saying a word. Christopher leaning back and silent has the teacher share for him based on her current knowledge.

Shihti	*I'm doing really good concentrating today*
Bella	*I like to draw a lot*
Monica	*[pass]*
Bobby	*I like playing with my brother*
Teacher	*But you don't have a brother*
Bobby	*[sits in silence]…I like playing with my sister*
Teacher	*[shakes her head]…I like playing*
Austin	*My name is Austin and I like spiders. [Loud confident voice with a gleaming smile]*
Cameron	*[soft voice and asked three times to repeat]*
Sienna	*I like to play princess with Mia*
Teacher	*We are going to choose some activities. We need to pick a volunteer to help us. [Teachers select and comment how they are looking for people they have not had help them before].*

The students break the circle, some stay seat; others jump with their hands in their air trying to gain the attention of their teacher. Chaos emerges within the excitement. The students disperse off to their selected activities. These activities are all students focused and student choice.

Mia	*not fair [imitates crying with her bottom lip scrunch up and wiping her eyes. She turns the acting on as quick as she stops it.] Sienna already had a turn [observant of own close friend and her activities].*

Figure 30. Bashir has a timer.

Figure 31. Bashir asks the teacher about the timer.

Bashir   *[problem solving how to get a timer to work, approaches two classmates to problem solve together (Figure 30). He then moves away and head towards the teacher.] What is this? [has timer in his hands and approaches the teacher, see Figure 31.] How does this work?*

Figure 32. Bashir is still considering the timer.

15 minutes later, see Figure 32. [persistence to problem solve?]

Figure 33. Bashir discusses timer with classmates.

[35 minutes later Bashir comes to me one on one where I am working with Gabriel]

129

Bashir   *This is my timer. It doesn't work anymore. I have to do it [wind the timer and then forces it to count down].*

Figure 34. Bashir shows another classmate.

[55 minutes later]

Figure 35. Shantell alone at reading table.

Figure 36. Shantell flicking through picture book.

Shantell	[reading by herself at the reading table (Figure 35). She flicks rapidly through the pages, looking at the pictures, her interest is not maintained in the book beyond 20 seconds (Figure 36)] [She looks at the key word that have been prepared on the paddle pop sticks]
Narelle	What do you do with these?
Shantell	They are our special words
Narelle	What do you do with them?
Shantell	You use them to find the word in the book, [demonstrates quickly, again loses interest and runs away]

Five minutes later S returns to NL's side, this time she is ready to talk and wants attention. Her personality glows more this time, confidence beaming in her smile and body language.

Shantell	So you want to make something with me? [referring to the creating and making table that is nearby]

Figure 37. Jaden & Austin.

Figure 38. Jaden & Austin looking at Australian song book.

131

Jayden	*I see a monster [pointing at the page of the book]*
Austin	*No that's a bird's eye [Looking at the Australian Song book]*

[All three boys are draped over the table, holding up the large book with double pages open to recall animals they can see.]

Jayden	*Kangaroo*
Austin	*Rat*
Jayden	*Bird*
Austin	*Butterfly*

Figure 39. Gabriele working at whiteboard.

Gabriele	*[working alone at the whiteboard he is playing guess what word a modification of hangman with himself. He draws lines that will hold a letter. Then he says a word, and then tries to sound it out and spell the word. He then finds magnetic versions of the letters in the tray below the whiteboard to match his writing of the letters. He's content working by himself, every now and then he rests and sits down before jumping back up with energy to continue working on his words. He's writing with a purple whiteboard marker and interacts with peers when they stop by him but never worried about being disturbed from what he is doing. Once his peer leave he continues with what he is doing.*

Figure 40. Gabriele places magnetic letters.

Figure 41. Gabriele writes between magnetic letters.

NL   *What are you doing?*

Gabriele *space space space sssssss [he says these while pointing to the whiteboard. He looks at my notes and sees I have written his name as Gabriel.] I'll spell my name for you. G a g r I e l. There now you have it right.*

I'm writing slug
Slug, [sounds out] "u"
Gabriele   *[He writes slg and then looks at me and says] slug*
NL   *[I sound slug out for him]...s l u g*
Gabriele   *So I'm missing a word [letter]*

[He rubs out his writing and write s l _ g]

[Then adds U with his writing, and follows to find a magnetic U in the box below].

Gabriele   *Do you know what a slug looks like?*
NL   *Yes*
Gabriele   *it leaves slim everywhere. Can you draw it for me?*
NL   *[draws] Now you*
Gabriele   *[draws his slug on the board]. Now I'm going to draw swimming.*

[30 minutes later, outside]

Figure 42. Mia with 'chocolate cake'.

Nicholas   *Want to come to our food?*
Mia   *chocolate cake...do you want some [come with a saucepan filled with san and a lid on top. hold it with two hands up to my face like you can smell it fresh from the oven] That's dessert!*
Frank   *But you have to eat other things first...*
Nicholas   *Yeah, dinner first*
Mia   *This is chicken and chips*

Figure 43. Sharing 'food'.

Figure 44. I'm painting.

Figure 45. Painting.

I'm painting [pouring water over a pine stump then continues to speak in a baby voice with syllables that are unrecognizable. This continues for two minutes before I walk away]

Figure 46. I'm blowing bubbles.

Frank   Blowing bubble

Other student No, you're not, you're drinking the water [voice of a peer]

Frank   No, I'm not, I'm blowing out, not sucking in.

Figure 47. Siena's 'lights'.

Figure 48. Careful, Mia.

Siena   *These are lights. Careful Mia [as Mia tries to walk through the sandcastle lined up along the sand pit ledge. It seems she doesn't like the attention Sienna has and on purpose walks through the sand castles. Sienna pauses...] doesn't matter I can fix it. [She rebuilds; active problem solving and moving on with her building]*

Siena   *It's going to be dark in here if there are wrecked*

Figure 49. Siena rebuilds her 'lights'.

Figure 50. Siena.

CONCLUSION

In this chapter the case presented that highlights how narratives without children can assist in investigating practice and contribute to reflective practice. Focus has been on image based methods and capturing narratives voices of children. The case illuminates how a research project on a program indivertibly created narratives on children. In the school readiness project documentation produced by the children, observation on the children, and assessment materials created on the children are used as data sources juxtaposed with interviews by teachers of the children and policymakers who address children's education needs. A varying approach of observation sees image based methods being employed as the researcher generates digital images of the learning activity while capturing the dialogue of the young people. This is seen as a creative way to present narratives on children and builds off the work of Margaret Carr (2001). In working this way contemporary approached to integrating digital technology to generate data is employed.

REFERENCES

Ainscow, M., Carrington, S., Deppeler, J., Engelbrecht, P., Forlin, C., Hay, T., Mumba, P. (2004, May). *Using visual images to make sense of inclusion education: An interactive symposium based on experiences in five countries.* Paper presented at the conference of Inclusive and Supportive Education Congress International Special Education Conference Inclusion: Celebrating Diversity, Glasgow, Scotland.

Bach, H. (1998). *A visual narrative concerning curriculum, girls, photography etc.* Edmonton, Alberta, Canada: Qual Institute Press.

Berger, J., & Mohr, J. (1982). *Another way of telling.* New York, NY: Pantheon.

Berman, H., Ford-Gilboe, M., Moutrey, B., & Cekic, S. (2001). Portraits of pain and promise: A photographic study of Bosnian youth. *Canadian Journal of Nursing Research, 32*(4), 21–41.

Burnard, P. (2001). *Using image-based techniques in researching pupil perspectives: How the deepest discoveries require sometimes the briefest expression.* Paper presented at the conference of Consulting Pupils about Teaching and Learning – a workshop, University of Cambridge, Cambridge, UK. Retrieved January 2, 2008 from http://www.esrc.ac.uk/my-esrc/grants/L139251006/outputs/read/6bea25d4-8ace-4d43-8c73-92378c92af21

Carr, M. (2001). *Assessment in early childhood settings: Learning stories.* London: Paul Chapman Publishing.

Carr, M. (1998, September). *A project for assessing children's experiences in early childhood settings.* Paper presented at the conference of the European Conference on Quality in Early Childhood Setting. Santiago de Compostela, Spain.

Carrington, S., & Holm, K. (2005). Students direct inclusive school development: A secondary school case study. *The Australasian Journal of Special Education, 29*(20), 155–171.

Chronaki, A., & Jess, K. (2002). Visual images from the lives of immigrant pupils in maths classrooms. In P. Valero & O. Skovsmose (Eds.), *Proceeding of the 3rd International Mathematics Education and Society Conference* (pp. 1–5). Copenhagen: Centre for Research in Learning Mathematics.

Clandinin, D. J., & Connelly, F. M. (2000). *Narrative inquiry: Experience and story in qualitative research.* San Francisco, CA: Jossey-Bass.

Clandinin, D. J., & Connelly, F. M. (1994). Telling teaching stories. *Teacher Education Quarterly, 21*(1), 145–158.

Collier, J. (1967). *Visual anthropology: Photography as a research method.* New York, NY: Holt, Rinehart and Winston.

Daniels, D. (2004). They need to know where they came from to appreciate where they are going to – Visual commentary of informal settlement women on motherhood. *Journal of Cultural and African Women Studies, 5.* Retrieved June 23, 2006 from http://www.africaknowledgeproject.org/index.php/jenda/article/view/97

Eber, D. E. (2002). The student's construction of artistic truth in digital images. In C. Beardon & L. Malmborg (Eds.), *Digital creativity: A reader* (pp. 45–60). Lisse: Swets & Zeitlinger.

Ellum, L. (2005). Digital storytelling as a teaching tool. *Fine Print, 28*(2), 1–6.

Ewald, W., & Lightfoot, A. (2001). *I wanna take me a picture-teaching. photography and writing to children.* Boston, MA: Center for Documentary Studies (in association with Beacon Press).

Fasoli, L. (2003). Reading photographs of young children: Looking at practices. *Contemporary Issues in Early Childhood, 4*(1), 32–47.

Gough, D. (2011). Strapped for cash, parents push for two years' prep. *The Age.* Retrieved June 27, 2014 from http://www.theage.com.au/victoria/strapped-for-cash-parents-push-for-two-years-prep-20110827-1jfs3.html#ixzz35nE3wSB4

Grauer, K., Irwin, R., Cosson, A., & Wilson, S. (2001). Images for understanding: Snapshots of learning through the arts. *International Journal of Education and the Arts, 2*(9). Retrieved June 21, 2006 from http://www.ijea.org/v2n9/

Hamilton, J. (2004). Digital camera explained. *Classroom Magazine,* 24–25.

Harper, D. (1998). An argument for visual sociology. In J. Prosser (Ed.), *Image-based research: A sourcebook for qualitative researchers* (pp. 24–41). London: Falmer Press.

Harrington, C., & Lindy, I. (1998, May). *The use of reflexive photography in the study of the freshman year experience.* Paper presented at the conference of the Annual Conference of the Indiana Association for Institutional Research, Nashville, IN.

Henderson, B., Meier, D., & Perry, G. (2004). Voices of practitioners: Teacher research in early childhood education. *YC Young Children, 59*(2), 94–100.

Inkpen, K. (2001). *Designing handheld technologies for kids.* Proceedings of Conference on Human Factors in Computing Systems, Seattle, WA.

Lemon, N. (2007). Take a photograph: Teacher reflection through narrative. *Journal of Reflective Practice, 8*(2), 177–191.

Lemon, N. (2008). Looking through the lens of a camera in the early childhood classroom (pp. 21–52). In J. Moss (Ed.), *Research education: Visually-digitally-spatially.* Rotterdam, the Netherlands: Sense Publishers.

Loeffler, T. A. (2004). *A picture is worth… capturing meaning and facilitating connections using outdoor education students' photographs.* Paper presented for the conference of the International Outdoor Education Research Conference, Latrobe University, Bendigo.

Meadows, D. (2006). Free photographic omnibus. *DG Magazine, 122,* 88–91.

Miles, S., & Kaplan, I. (2005). Using images to promote reflection: An action research study in Zambia and Tanzania. *Journal of Research in Special Educational Needs, 5*(2), 77.

Moran, M. J., & Tegano, D. W. (2005). Moving toward visual literacy: Photography as a language of teacher inquiry. *Early Childhood Research and Practice, 7*(1), 1–23.

Moss, J. (Ed.) (2008). *Educational researchers working – visually-digitally-spatially.* Rotterdam, the Netherlands: Sense Publications.

Moss, J. (2003). *Picture this: Visual narrative as a source for understanding diversity in our classrooms.* Melbourne: Festival against Racism in Education.

Moss, J., & Hay, T. (2004). Local knowing: Narrative inquiry and the teacher-researcher. In J. Moss (Ed.), *Invitations and inspirations: Pathways to successful teaching.* Carlton South, Australia: Curriculum Corporation.

Packard, B. W., Ellison, K. L., & Sequenzia, R. (2004). Show and tell: Photo-Interviews with urban adolescent girls. *International Journal of Education and the Arts, 5*(3). Retrieved June 21, 2006 from http://ijea.org/v5n3

Pink, S. (2001). *Visual ethnography: Images, media and representation in research.* London: Sage Publications.

Prosser, J. (Ed.). (1998). *Image-based research: A sourcebook for qualitative researchers.* London: Falmer Press.

Punch, S. (2002, August). Research with children: The same or different from research with adults? *Childhood, 9,* 321–341.

Ramella, M., & Olmos, G. (2005). *Participant authored audiovisual stories (PAAS): Giving the camera away or giving the camera a way?* (Social Research Methods Qualitative Series 10). London: London School of Economics and Political Science.

Roxburgh, M., & Kasunic, J. L. (2005). Looking for limits in a world of excess. *Visual: Design: Scholarship: Research Journal of the Australian Graphic Design Association, 1*(1), 1–14.

Sanborn, R. D., & Giardino, A. P. (2014). Family well-being and social environments: Correlations within childhood. *Journal of Applied Research on Children: Informing Policy for Children at Risk, 5*(1), I Article 1. Retrieved June 27, 2014 from http://digitalcommons.library.tmc.edu/childrenatrisk/vol5/iss1/1

Schön, D. (1987). *Educating the reflective practitioner.* Paper presented at the 1987 meeting of the American Educational Research Association, Washington, DC. Retrieved August 29, 2006 from http://resources.educ.queensu.ca/ar/schon87.htm

Schratz-Hadwich, B., Walker, R., & Egg, P. (2004, December). *Photo evaluation: A participatory ethnographic research and evaluation tool in child care and education.* Paper presented at the conference of the Australian Association for Research in Education, The University of Melbourne, Australia.

Sharpies, M. (2002). The design of personal mobile technologies for lifelong learning. *Computers and Education, 34,* 177–193.

Swan, K., van't Hooft, M., Kratcoski, A., & Unger, D. (2005). Uses and effects of mobile computing devices in K-8 classrooms. *Journal of Research on Technology in Education, 38*(1), 99–113.

Van House, N. A., Davis, M., Takhteyev, Y., Ames, M., & Finn, M. (2004). *The social uses of personal photography: Methods for projecting future imaging applications.* Berkeley, CA: University of California. Retrieved June 23, 2006 from http://people.ischool.berkeley.edu/~vanhouse/van_house_et_al_2004b.pdf

Walker, R., & Adelman, C. (1975). *A guide to classroom observation.* London: Methuen and Co Ltd.

Warren, S. (2002). Show me how it feels to work here: Using photography to research organizational aesthetics. *Ephemera: Critical Dialogues on organization, 2*(3), 224–245.

Worden, S. (2003, October). *Sight or insight: Accounting for the visual in design research.* Paper presented for Emerging Research Cultures in Design Education, Curtin University of Technology, Australia. Retrieved June 23, 2006 from http://www.designresearchsociety.org/docs-procs/ded3/d_final_paper/d_10.pdf

Ziller, R. C. (1990). *Photographing the self: Methods for observing personal orientations.* Newbury Park, CA: Sage.

Narelle Lemon
La Trobe University

ABOUT THE AUTHORS

Susanne Garvis is a professor of child and youth studies at the University of Gothenburg, Sweden. She is also an adjunct professor at Griffith University, Australia. Her publications include narrative methodology and approaches with young children, families and teachers.

Elin Eriksen Ødegaard is a professor at the *Centre of Educational Research*, Bergen University College, and a visiting professor at University of Tromsø, Norway. Her publications include narrative research about children and teachers, cultural formation in kindergarten and how kindergarten as a complex arena shape conditions for meaning-making and local pedagogical practice.

Narelle Lemon is a senior lecturer at La Trobe University, Melbourne, Australia. Her research agenda is focused on engagement and participation in the areas of teacher capacity building and cultural organisations in galleries, museums and other alternative education settings, arts education, social media for professional development including Twitter, and women in academia.

CPSIA information can be obtained at www.ICGtesting.com
Printed in the USA
BVOW11*0851130515

399243BV00005B/14/P